BEYOND BOOZE

Stepping Into Sobriety

BY
ALEX HYNDMAN HILL
#1 International Best Seller

BEYOND BOOZE

Stepping Into Sobriety

Beyond Booze: Stepping Into Sobriety

1st Edition. 2024 -V3

ASIN: 978-0-6459069-0-5 (Amazon Kindle)
ISBN: 978-0-6459069-1-2 (Amazon) PAPERBACK
ISBN: 978-0-6459069-3-6 (Amazon) HARDCOVER
ISBN: 978-0-6459069-2-9 (Ingram Spark) PAPERBACK
ISBN: 978-0-6459069-4-3 (Ingram Spark) HARDCOVER
ISBN: 978-0-6459069-0-5 (Smashwords)

CONTACT THE AUTHOR:
Business Name: Hyndman Hill Media
Author Website: www.alexhyndmanhill.com
Email: hello@alexhyndmanhill.com
Font Type: Adobe Garamond Pro
Font Size: 12pt

Table of Contents

About The Author

Alex is an international journalist with over twenty years of experience in TV, radio, and print media. She has anchored news and sports programs around the world and written articles for publications across the globe. Alex has now added author to her long list of achievements with her first book inspired by her personal journey into sobriety.

After her marriage broke down, Alex moved back to Australia with her two young children. She found herself turning to alcohol to cope with stress, anxiety, and depression. However, when the father of her children passed away, her drinking escalated, and her children witnessed her at her worst. This was the wake-up call Alex needed to make a change.

Today, Alex is not just a journalist but also a beacon of hope for those struggling with alcohol. She helps people see that not drinking is the new normal. She shares her story openly and honestly, making her a relatable and trustworthy figure for those who are battling their own issues with alcohol.

Alex's mission is to show others that a fulfilling life without alcohol is not just possible but within their reach. She talks about the positive changes that came from giving up alcohol and models this for others to do in their own lives. Her story is a testament to the power of resilience and the possibility of transformation, making her an inspiration to many.

Dedication

For Olivia & Alfie, you are my reason

And For Warren, my love

"

Rock bottom became
the solid foundation
on which I rebuilt my
life.

JK Rowling

Introduction

I knew I drank too much, but if I had to pinpoint a moment that made me realise my drinking was out of control and had to stop, that was the moment.

The stairs incident was over two years ago now. It was the last time I was drunk, and it was the start of me finally getting sober and telling my story.

That story starts when I found alcohol in my teens.

At first, I drank to fit in.

I moved from Adelaide to London when I was 16, and all the kids I became friends with drank and smoked. We bought litre bottles of cider for a few pounds, and packs of ten cigarettes, and hung out in parks or at friends' places when their parents weren't around.

I then drank my way through university.

Drinking at the student bar was part of everyday life, and it was so cheap that we never thought twice about buying drinks all night.

When I graduated and got my first job as a newsreader, I drank with all my friends who worked in the media. I normally presented the breakfast show, which meant work was over by midday, and that's when the drinking at lunchtime began. There were endless work events, late nights, and early mornings.

I burnt the candle at both ends.

When I look back now, I am filled with remorse and shame. I can't quite believe how this behaviour was normalised and how enthusiastically I embraced it. It was as though I was encouraged to drink at every turn and I seized every opportunity. Every social event revolved around drinking; there was alcohol in the office, at office parties, and at work events.

Every social occasion with my friends began and ended with drinking.

I wasn't around alcohol or this type of drinking until I hit my late teens and early twenties. But when the floodgates opened, I turned on the tap and was quickly hooked.

While some of my friends and colleagues managed to moderate or at least seemed to know when to call it a night, I had no off switch.

Once I started, there was no stopping me.

I fell madly in love with drinking and ignored all the red flags. I was in deep water; nothing was going to discourage me from diving head-first into drinking like there was no tomorrow.

Working as a journalist in London was synonymous with drinking.

Drinking, at least in my eyes, was all part of the game, part of the networking I had to do, part of what I needed to do to fit in and get ahead. I wanted to be like Carrie Bradshaw and Bridget Jones. They drank like fish, so I did too. I loved the sophisticated image I thought I was portraying by ordering strong cocktails, learning about fancy old wine, and ordering the right bottle at restaurants.

I went from radio newsreader to National TV presenter, fronting shows in the UK on Sky News, Sky Sports, ITV, and Channel 5.

I should be clear though; I don't think this happened because I drank. I may have put myself out there more because I had dutch courage, from drinking. But honestly, I think I was extremely lucky that it didn't derail my entire career. I think I got away with it because I was a high-functioning people pleaser.

I always showed up, even if I did smell like cigarettes and booze from the night before.

Life went on like this for over a decade.

During this period, I pumped the brakes only a handful of times.

The first time lasted a few months. I was training for the London Marathon and was terrified of finishing last so I stopped drinking in the lead-up to the big day. I trained as hard as my unfit body would allow and ran it in a decent enough time. Straight afterward, I hobbled into the news studio to talk about the experience and then headed to the pub for way too many gin and tonics to celebrate.

The next time was when I landed in the main national Newsreaders seat on the UK's ITV News.

My boyfriend worked in the newsroom too and warned me I shouldn't risk being seen tumbling out of a cab into work straight from the night before if I didn't want to end up in the papers for the wrong reasons. I cut out the drinking, stayed away from alcohol when we got engaged, and planned our wedding. I hadn't had a drink in four months when we got married and consequently found out I was pregnant on honeymoon.

Fast forward 20 years and I'm now a mum of two living back in Australia.

I moved back home with my kids who are now 11 and 13 years old. Their father Geoff and I got a divorce after five years of marriage.

My drinking wasn't the reason we broke up, but it didn't help our relationship.

Rather than giving up drinking when I became a mum, I went back to my old drinking habits right after my children were born, and it escalated when I became a single mum.

I drank at home on my own when they were in bed. I drank so regularly that the kids, who were about 5 and 6 at the time, would remind me to stop at the bottle shop on the way home from school or kindergarten.

I knew I was drinking too much but I'd always find a way to justify it.

There'd be an article saying red wine was good for you or that some vodka or tequila creation was some fabulous celebrity's drink of choice. I told myself it wasn't a problem, but every time I felt the shame creeping in I googled, "Am I an alcoholic?"

It was clear I was drinking at dangerous levels.

I'd drink when I went out for lunch with friends, or after school pick up at the pub. At this stage, I'd have at least a couple of gin and tonics and a bottle of wine a night on my own; way more than the recommended amount.

The Australian health guidelines say women should have no more than ten standard drinks a week or four standard drinks a day. That's the equivalent of a couple of small glasses of wine, with about half a glass of wine being one standard drink.

Turns out I was far from alone in drinking at levels like this.

After the pandemic hit, day-drinking was more widely accepted and even encouraged. Mixing up margaritas in the middle of the day seemed like a fun way to get through the never-ending lockdown. Everyone else appeared to be doing it too, alongside watching their sourdough starters rise. Booze was now available on demand, delivered in minutes along with the groceries, minus the toilet paper.

Good times.

While for some, it was a short-lived distraction, for those who were already abusing alcohol or dependent on it, this was a recipe for disaster.

The number of middle-aged Australian women now drinking above the recommended safe amount was already quickly catching up to men before lockdown. Now researchers say women my age are drinking more than they have in decades and are doing so at "increasingly risky levels".

A 2022 study by the Menzies School of Health Research and the Centre for Alcohol Policy Research led by Mia Miller, revealed around 21 percent of women aged between 45 and 60 consume alcohol at "binge drinking" levels. This group consume more than four standard drinks in one session "with the aim of getting drunk". The study, published in the Drug and Alcohol Review, is just one of many pointing to why drinking habits like mine should be seen as anything but safe or normal.

According to the International Agency for Research on Cancer, there is no safe level of alcohol consumption.

It is classified as a Group 1 carcinogen and is recognised as the "second greatest preventable cause of drug-related death and hospitalisation in Australia," just behind smoking.

The National Health and Medical Research Council also states there is never a completely safe amount of alcohol, and stresses drinking any alcohol "can cause harm to the person who drinks and sometimes to those around them".

According to the Australian Department of Health, 6,000 people die each year because of alcohol abuse.

What I've learnt in writing this book is that addiction doesn't discriminate.

The image of a dishevelled park bench dweller swigging from a bottle disguised inside a brown paper bag is not what addiction looks like. Addicts can present themselves as fully functioning and hold down high-powered, well-paid jobs while masking the truth of their addiction.

Luckily, though, attitudes are changing.

Local governments are investing in health-led approaches to dealing with public drunkenness. There are more facilities to help people suffering from addiction to alcohol, and this book is one of hundreds being written on the subject.

I'm just one of thousands and thousands of women who have hit rock bottom and clawed my way out.

It may be that you've had enough of alcohol, and you simply don't like the taste or its effects anymore.

You hear the champagne cork pop, and just can't stomach it.

If you've had enough of the hangovers and dusty mornings, or don't like being out of control anymore, then you're not alone.

Many women my age are also finding alcohol affects them differently, now they're in perimenopause or menopause.

Australia has long had a reputation for heavy drinking, but there is a turning point on the horizon.

Alcohol consumption is on the decline, particularly among Aussie teens.

According to the Australian Bureau of Statistics, there's been a sharp decline in the number of teenagers drinking alcohol. Factors affecting their choices are cited as costs and a growing awareness of the harm alcohol can do.

Teenagers are more aware of the negative impact and realising alcohol can have a long-lasting effect on their health and wellbeing.

Studies have also shown a steady growth in the low or non-alcoholic drinks market.

More people are revelling in the benefits of booze-free beers, and joining the growing sober movement without the stigma attached to choosing not to drink like never before.

When I quit booze, non-alcoholic drinks were my saviour.

I needed something to take the edge off.

Something to stop me craving having a real drink in my hand, and alcohol -free drinks were a huge help. Along with having a handy alternative, I started to document how I was feeling, and what was helping me get through the days when I normally would have propped myself up with booze.

I found ways to cope.

What I'm here to share is what I needed at the start of my journey.

I needed to hear all the reasons I should give up, break the cycle and get through the days that followed.

I needed the tools to navigate the first hours, days, and the first week without a drink.

I needed someone to tell me what to say when people asked me why I wasn't drinking.

I needed to know what to do to get through that first event where everyone seemed to be drinking, and I was suddenly exposed and felt alone in not drinking.

I needed to know what came after that final drunken night.

The day I decided to quit is still clear in my mind.

The shame and regret and the fear in the pit of my stomach.

A few weeks earlier I had been out with some other mums, and we carried on drinking when we got back to my friend's place. My kids were there when they'd normally be home in bed with a babysitter on duty, and they saw us all drinking until the early hours. When I finally took them home, stumbling up the hill with no shoes on, they were confused and upset. When we got in the door, they saw me fall over. Luckily, I was only bruised but at 9 and 10 years old, my children were old enough to tell me that they didn't like it.

They needed me, and it scared them to see me like that.

My dependence on alcohol and poor mental state had been hugely affected by our family situation at the time. Their Dad was still living in London and had been sick for a while. He'd been diagnosed with leukaemia a few years after we divorced, and I'd been drinking more and more to try and drown out the horrible thoughts inside my head. Geoff was in hospital in London and with COVID restrictions still in place, there wasn't a lot I could do.

I drank to cope with my guilt about having moved so far away with Alfie and Olivia, and I drank to deal with my devastation for the children losing their father.

The only coping mechanism I had invested any time in was drinking.

I turned to alcohol for everything.

So, looking back, it was no surprise that I drank to cope with the grief when Geoff died.

I drank a lot.

It didn't help anything of course.

I stopped drinking on the 1st of October 2021, a few weeks after Geoff passed away, and about a week after the falling down the stairs incident.

It was when my children needed me most, but my emotional state was a disaster. I was consumed by grief and couldn't stop crying. I had been drinking to try and numb the pain, but I finally knew it had to end. I had to work through my grief and support my children through theirs. If nothing else, I wanted Alfie and Olivia not to have to worry that they were going to lose another parent when they'd just lost their dad.

I channelled my energy into getting through the first few months of sobriety by researching alcohol abuse and dependence, writing articles, and posting on social media. I wanted to be vocal about giving up alcohol, and I wanted to find people like me who had gone through this and come out the other side. I needed new role models, and new people to look up to. I needed to find people who didn't drink.

I started to lose weight, and my face shape even changed. I started exercising every day and my skin was suddenly glowing. I started sleeping better and was a little nicer to be around in the morning.

I cursed all those happy morning people I'd rolled my eyes at for years.

I found new friends who didn't drink all the time.

The experts were right: exercise, sleep, and drinking water instead of attempting to hydrate myself with gin really did work.

I found my motivation.

I started writing this book, landed gigs on radio and TV, and realised how much my drinking had been holding me back.

I also became more present with my kids and my partner, Warren.

We met in 2018 and had bonded over our shared love of fine wine, and nice restaurants.

He was initially worried about how me quitting drinking might affect our relationship.

He told me he would miss sharing a bottle of wine with me and chatting around the fire pit in the evening. But, having seen me at my worst, he knew quitting drinking was the right choice. Warren has supported me the whole way and has spent long periods alcohol-free as well. It took a little getting used to, but now we share a bottle of non-alcoholic wine, or he mixes me a fake gin and tonic, and we still sit out by the fire and chat like we used to.

We got married in 2022 and served non-alcoholic bubbles at the reception on the beach in Noosa.

We danced with the kids and smiled all night. I didn't make a fool of myself, didn't have a hangover the next day, and most importantly, didn't fall in front of the children.

I have started to forgive myself, move past the shame, and work on blaming myself less.

There were times when I thought I'd failed my children, I thought my career had failed, my marriage to their father had failed, and I'd failed at being happy. The only thing it turns out I'd failed at was recognising sooner how much of a damaging impact drinking was having on my life.

When I cut alcohol out, everything changed, and the feeling of failure started to go away.

It hasn't all been easy, and it's taken a lot of work, but I've stopped feeling embarrassed about not being able to drink, and now realise I have so much more power than I ever could have imagined.

Reflecting on my alcohol abuse, I think a lot of the feelings I had about drinking came from societal expectations around alcohol. The pressures and the expectation to go out and have a drink, meant constantly battling to do so "responsibly" and then feeling ashamed if we fail to stay in control.

While I was lucky to have the support of my family, when I decided to give up, I still needed to find my own way, carve my own path, and work out what I wanted life to look like.

My road to sobriety hasn't been smooth sailing; it's been bumpy as hell, and I've had days when I've felt totally alone.

Surprisingly, there have been many times I've questioned my decision to give up drinking and wondered if I'd ever go back to drinking one day.

I know the best version of me is sober and that alcohol only takes away.

Finding others like me was one of the most important things; I couldn't recommend it more.

Connecting with people who knew they drank too much and found it hard to quit, stopped me from feeling so alone.

Making new connections with people who don't drink has shown me that there is a different way to live life, and I'm not the only one who initially found it hard to see that.

Hearing other people's stories encouraged me to write this.

I've talked to experts who work in recovery and addiction and now know there is so much help out there, I've shared everything that helped me here.

The first year of giving up alcohol changed me in ways I could never have imagined, and I know that change is possible.

It's the best decision I ever made.

I wanted to give back, to help and offer support to anyone who feels the way I did.

I know what it is to feel like a failure and alone, stuck in a cycle of drinking and unable to see a way out.

This is a guide to a life beyond booze.

There is no shame in this book about the relationship you have with alcohol or the trouble you've faced trying to break free.

It's about me facing up to my shame, shining a light on it and watching it die.

After all, shame dies when you expose it to the light.

A typical night at university

66

Shame dies when you expose it to the light

CHAPTER 1

Addicted

Eleven-forty PM, February 2016

Jan Juc, Victoria, Australia

I swipe right and immediately get a notification.

You have a match.

My phone is much more excited about this than I am. Playing on dating apps is just another thing to do, another way to pass the time. It's time that I have so much of now, especially in these hours after the kids have gone to bed.

I have the whole night stretching out ahead of me alone, somewhere between drunk and blackout drunk again. I lay in my massive, super king-sized bed, draped in girly pink linen sheets, squinting to see the bio of the latest guy I've matched with on Tinder.

I don't know what I was thinking when I moved here. On paper it's an idilyic beach town, a couple of hours south of Melbourne. In reality, this is a place where happy families come, not newly single mums. This is where dads who surf raise their little groms, and where families spend weekends on the beach watching their kids do nippers or surf. This is not where thirty-somethings come to start over. But this is where

I am, and this is why I'm swiping erratically. I'm trying to find someone to spend time with, someone vaguely suitable or even slightly interesting. This is not an easy task in this town full of families and devoid of nightlife.

When I decided to move I wanted something different to London, somewhere I could be alone with my thoughts and work out what's next. I asked myself:

Where do I want my life to be now the fairy-tale life I had is over?

When I was married and living with Geoff, I was still drinking like this, but he was there. My addiction was always there, but now it's having a field day, and I'm drinking myself into a stupor at far more regular intervals. Now I'm unsupervised; no adults are around to keep an eye on me, and no one will walk through the door, pick me up and take care of me.

I'm in charge, and I have to keep two little kids alive, and no one is going to help.

As well as searching for a life completely different to the one I had in London I moved here to be closer to my family. But my Mum has her own life and doesn't appear to know how to talk about the fact that I'm a mess. My sister has her own marital problems to deal with, so I'm still alone. Just me, my drinking habit, and cliched late-night swiping.

I've spent endless nights on this dating app, mostly to fill the time, but it feels addictive too.

I have no problem getting addicted to things that are bad for me.

I'm addicted to swiping and the idea of possibility, even though I've pretty much resigned myself to the fact that this is not where I will find husband number two.

I stare at my phone and scroll through the messages: endless profiles of guys holding fish, some posing next to tigers, and so many surfing pictures.

I land on Travis and think to myself, *he'll do*. Suitably flirty messages, close by and someone who might be described as a "fuck boy".

Not anyone who will be around long enough to meet the kids.

I flick him a message. "You want to hook up tomorrow night?"

He replies quickly.

"Yes, my Queen. Meet you on the beach at 7."

My Queen? Yuck.

If I hadn't drunk two bottles of wine, I wouldn't entertain this conversation, but I'm too far gone.

Drunk, lonely and looking for a distraction in any way, shape or form.

So, the following night I leave the kids with a babysitter and head for the beach.

My footprints leave wet, dark imprints as I walk along the stretch of sand just a few meters from where we now call home. As I look behind me, I watch my footprints disappear as the waves lap onto the shore and erase all evidence of my existence.

Would it matter if I wasn't here anymore? I wonder.

They would probably be happier without me.

I spot Travis on the bench under the fir trees dotted along the foreshore. Crossing the denser sand, my feet sink into the cool layers underneath. He doesn't look totally different from his picture online, but, most importantly, he has two bottles of wine and plastic glasses resting on the bench next to him.

He stands up to greet me with an embrace and a peck on the cheek. His gentlemanly manner clashed with my image of him after last night's bout of flirty and increasingly dirty messages.

"I didn't know if you'd fancy white or bubbles, so I brought both," he explains.

"Let's start with the bubbles," I suggest.

He pops the cork and proffers me a glass, and we attempt to chink the plastic against each other.

"Cheers"; he winks.

A knowing look passes between us; we both know where this night is going.

I already hate myself for what's about to happen. I can't embrace the idea that I'm out here having fun and being single. It all feels so desperate and pointless. I feel nauseous as the cool liquid starts to churn inside my empty stomach. We sit and watch other couples strolling along the beach as dusk turns the sky pink and attempt to make small talk.

He has four kids. Four?! And a wife.

"But we've been separated for six months now," he reassures me.

At this point, it probably wouldn't have made a difference if I were honest. If he'd said he was still with her, or they were trying to work things out, that is where my self-respect has landed, right in the gutter with my mind.

"My ex is in London", I explain. "The kids and I are here now to be closer to my family. I needed the help, so ..." I trail off. He's looking into my eyes.

The wind catches strands of my hair, sweeping across my cheek. He gently brushes them behind my ear and leans in to kiss me. I let him, and I'm only slightly aware of how we must look like teenagers on a park bench. Like a couple, I'd glimpse and think, *get a room*.

The four glasses of wine I had while getting ready, and the two glasses of champagne now mean I've reached the point of no return.

This is where the wrong decisions live.

This is where it all starts to go wrong.

This is where I lose control.

We gather up the remaining wine and glasses and head for his car. It's not the spot I'd choose, but at this point, I don't really care. We get in the back seat of his dark blue hatchback, and I straddle him.

We fumble around with each other's clothes, ignoring that people are still everywhere. They're walking close enough to the car to see but most quickly looking away, pretending not to see what we are blatantly doing in public.

What are you doing? My conscience shouts at me.

I've become accustomed to ignoring it, this voice in my head that speaks sense, the one I imagine is the little angel on my shoulder trying to battle the devil who keeps winning a one-sided fight. It's a battle where I am hurtling towards self-destruction. It's like in yoga when you're trying to lay down in Shavasana, and they say to acknowledge the thoughts that come into your head and let them pass away.

That's what I'm doing, watching the rational thoughts arrive, acknowledging them and then encouraging them to piss off.

My brain and my judgment are clouded once again by booze. I know how bad it is for me and the damage I'm doing.

I know.

I've read a lot about addiction and alcoholism and I get that I shouldn't feel shame, or blame myself for my drinking, but I can't help feeling like I have a choice in this. I feel like, despite all the scientific evidence to the contrary, I am choosing to abuse alcohol.

A part of me doesn't believe it's a disease, despite my Mum telling me for my entire life that it is categorically a condition that runs in our family. She cites it as one of the main reasons why her marriage to my father failed.

Even though I know Dad may have been a better father if he hadn't been such a big drinker, I honestly think it was his choice to drink. He chose it for the fun, he was the life and soul of the party. I loved that about him. I thought that my Mum cutting back on drinking with my dad was the reason they split up; she wasn't fun anymore, she had children and turned into the boring wife at home. I promised myself I'd never end up like that.

"Why didn't you just leave us with the nanny and go out and have fun with Dad?" I'd ask her unkindly, pushing for an argument.

I thought I knew it all, and I would never miss an opportunity to provoke her or try and make her feel bad to make myself feel better about my stupid choices.

"Someone had to get up through the night to check on you and your sister; someone had to be responsible and that someone was me. I don't think your father ever got up once in the night when you cried."

"Yeah, but wouldn't you guys have stayed together if you'd carried on like you were before we were born, if you'd still been his partner in crime, still gone out partying? Didn't you even consider it?" I poked her again.

"I wanted to be there for you two. I needed to take charge of everything," she said with a sigh.

She was done with this conversation.

"Look Alex, I loved your father, but he loved drinking and the pub more than he loved coming home to his family. I gave it a chance when I moved to Australia with him. I thought it would all be different. I wanted it to be, but he couldn't change. This is why I tell you to be careful: it's an awful, selfish disease that will wreck your life if you're not careful, so please, don't drink so much."

I was not listening.

As far as I could tell, from the time I'd spent with my father, he was fun.

I wanted to be like him, always out meeting new people in restaurants and bars, always happy. He wasn't an aggressive or sad drunk; he was himself, just more chatty and fun. I categorically did not want to be like my Mum. I didn't want to have kids and find that I had to choose between them and my relationship. I also didn't buy into the idea that the fun stopped when the kids arrived. Maybe if I did have kids I could have both; that's what I really wanted. I was determined to prove her wrong, so I ignored her advice and did my absolute best to do the opposite of what she had urged me to do. I drank like there was no tomorrow.

The question is whether or not I was fulfilling my genetic destiny by becoming addicted to alcohol or whether I had a choice.

My sister doesn't drink like I did and never has, so why was I the one who got the alcoholic gene?

Did I choose to lose control, or was control something that I could never possibly have over a substance as addictive as alcohol?

Neurosurgeon Andrew Huberman, speaking on The Huberman Lab Podcast, has identified a common trait among alcoholics, which I can relate to.

He explains that the way drinkers respond can determine whether or not there is the presence of a genetic predisposition to alcoholism.

According to Huberman, people who likely have alcoholism in their genes "typically experience an increase in alertness and mood when they drink." That's when compared to people who "after more than a couple of drinks, start to feel sedated," which he says demonstrates a lack of the predisposition.

It is always something that struck me about my drinking, I just felt better when I drank, more myself, more fun, more like my father on a night out. The next day, I suffered. The hangovers were sometimes intense, but I could always be counted on to start drinking again and find my way back to a tipsy equilibrium where I felt normal.

The feeling I got from alcohol meant that I chased it, sought it out and felt like it enhanced my life. If it had made me feel sick or sleepy, then that might not have been the case, and I could have been spared a whole lot of blackouts, crazy nights, poor choices and shameful memories.

What is the answer here, then? Did I fulfil my genetic destiny?

If you had told me that quitting alcohol entirely rather than being a low to moderate drinker was the only answer for me, then I would have been furious. When I was in the grip of my addiction, the last thing I wanted was to have my drink taken away. But if I'd never become addicted in the first place, things may have been different on all fronts.

What if, knowing that I had a predisposition to alcoholism, I was prescribed medication or counselling or had a mentor or sponsor?

I don't know what would have helped, but knowing what I know now, I wish I had asked for help before I descended into full-blown alcohol abuse.

I just wish I had asked for help.

One was never enough

> When I was in the grip of my addiction, the last thing I wanted was to have my drink taken away.

CHAPTER 2

Anxiety

Nine-fifteen AM, December 2013

Greenwich Park, London

They're both crying again, and I feel like crying too. It's fucking freezing. It's the middle of winter, and I'm pushing this stupid buggy with my two bawling babies through Greenwich Park. I can't feel my toes, and I want to cry too.

Pushing the pram over the crest of the frosty hill, I swig mulled wine out of my reusable coffee cup. I've already had two coffees laced with Baileys and have decided that I want to stay tipsy all day. I reckon I'll be happier and a better parent for it. That's what I'm telling myself anyway.

I wriggle my frozen fingers inside my gloves, wrapped tightly around the buggy handle as we head down the hill.

What would happen if I let go?

I nod as people give me looks of sympathy seeing my two red-faced, howling babies. Everyone can tell I'm shit at this.

I am shit at this.

This whole parenting thing is supposed to get easier after they get out of the newborn stage. Olivia is nearly three, and Alfie has just turned one. That's past newborn, right? I'm still stuck breastfeeding, up every hour, every single night, every single day, and as much as I love them, I hate it.

I hate this part.

I push the buggy faster up another hill, frustration fuelling my march.

My stomach clenches at the memory of our failed recent attempts just to let them cry it out, as the sleep nanny had prescribed.

"Just let them get tired; it's the only way they will learn to self-soothe."

She'd said it so matter of factly, like their crying didn't illicit an overwhelming physical response in me.

I spent the weekend sobbing into my pillow, listening to them both bawling their eyes out, calling for me over and over again. I was trying to be strong.

I'm not strong, I'm weak.

I failed at that, too.

I can't even get my own babies to sleep.

I shake my head, and the grey pom-poms on my beanie jiggle up and down as I try to shake out the thoughts invading my brain.

This life is not what I had imagined, it's not it at all.

Spotting the short queue inside the café, I breathe a sigh of relief and awkwardly manoeuvre the buggy inside.

I hate this stupid thing, I hate having to push them both around in it.

The warmth of the bustling café hits me almost immediately, and I struggle to take off my scarf, hat, gloves and jacket before I start sweating. I pile all my extra layers on top of the buggy, and I'm sure another meltdown will erupt as my children acclimate to the subtropical heat. They're dressed for snow, so as I try to shuffle along the line without bumping people carrying trays loaded precariously with hot chocolates, I unzip their snowsuits and whip off their hats.

Olivia looks up at me from the buggy with rosy-pink cheeks. Her shock of bright blonde hair sticks up off her head like she's been electrocuted. Alfie clutches three Hot Wheels cars in one hand and grabs his hat with the other.

I love you both. Honestly, I do.

I spot Rachel on the other side of the café. She's spooning whipped cream off the top of her hot chocolate and feeding it to her angelic little girl Bella. She looks up, either looking for me or feeling my eyes on her, and waves.

After I've ordered babyccinos and a double shot latte, I plonk myself down on the seat next to her and exhale dramatically.

"They really should be serving gin. It's basically lunch time." I lean in and plant a kiss on her cheek. "So, how are you?"

"I'm fine, darling. I'm worried about you. What did the shrink say?"

I cradle the mug in front of me with both hands, lift it to my lips, and slurp a mouthful of the steaming froth.

"Post-natal depression, just as you thought, my love. Anti-depressants and counselling for me," I add glibly.

"Did she say anything about drinking?"

"No. I mean, she asked if I was drinking more than normal, and I told her I wasn't, of course. I mean, what's normal anyway?."

Rachel screws up her nose in concern.

"Don't worry, I'll be careful," I lie.

Drinking has become my saviour at night. It's my crutch, my reward. It's the only thing I look forward to all day. Okay, it's what gets me through the day and it's what makes the evenings slightly more bearable.

My conversation with Rachel about drinking was the kind of conversation I had a lot during those early Mummy years, and lying to the psychiatrist was a given during that time too. I was not prepared to admit I drank too much because I was terrified I'd be told to stop.

The drinking, which I mostly thought I'd hidden, occasionally came up in conversation and I'd brush it off. I'd point to the fact we were all drinking. I knew I drank too much but with my marriage falling apart, I didn't know how else to cope. I wanted to block it out, to escape, to drown my anxiety. My anxiety reared its ugly head on a daily basis, but it went full-blown crazy whenever I decided to organise something outside of our usual basic routine.

For Olivia's third birthday, I had a panic attack because I'd planned a massive gathering at our house to celebrate with family and friends. I'd baked and catered and brought in helium tanks to fill hundreds of balloons. I'd overdone it, over-committed and over-invested in a birthday party for my toddler. I had a massive meltdown and started drinking heavily. My mental state was fragile, and my ability to cope with even the slightest inconvenience had dissipated.

"I just need to get these balloons done."

I glared at Geoff while saying this through gritted teeth, "If you could just help, that would be great."

He looked at me incredulously.

"You've lost it," he said and wandered off, leaving me on the floor surrounded by balloons and hyperventilating.

If I could stop all the stress, block out the dark thoughts, and find a way to release the hand that has worked its way inside my body, squeezing my lungs until I can't take a full breath.

Everywhere I turned, I found a reason to drink and took solace in the messages I found on TV, movies, books and social media that women like me drank.

I internalised the mantra *Mummy needs a drink* and thought it was perfectly normal for my kids to see me drinking alcohol like water.

Those birthday parties I threw were just another excuse to normalise my drinking, another excuse to order in lots of wine and drink for an entire day with my friends, get loose and pretend that the overwhelming anxiety of motherhood wasn't killing me.

Mummy Wine Culture was in its heyday, and if it needed an ambassador, I would have been perfect.

Hurrah For Gin was my go-to adult cartoon to share with friends. It featured a stick-figure parent who drank her way through parenting young children. I thought it was hilarious and thought it completely justified my behaviour. Everyone was doing it, so why would I even question it?

I had been sold the idea that drinking would help me relax and was an answer to yet another hard day. But, for someone like me, someone predisposed to alcoholism, it was an extraordinarily dangerous message. There is no way to know when enough is enough for someone like me, and no easy way to drink responsibly, even if I had attempted to. So drinking to unwind leads to getting drunk and my dependency on alcohol to cope grew.

The anxiety and depression that engulfed me after the birth of my two children was not helped by my drinking. It exacerbated my symptoms to a terrifying level. I was volatile and irrational and my actions when it came to alcohol were leading me down a very destructive path.

As well as the anxiety around blacking out and having to interrogate my friends and family to fill in the blanks, alcohol also stole my sleep. I was already struggling to get an hour or two a night. Drinking meant that I never had any deep or REM sleep, which plays a massive part in keeping stress and anxiety at bay.

I was constantly seeking the high that alcohol gave me, the dopamine that was released from the chemicals hitting my brain, so I kept drinking and crashing every single day.

I needed to find new ways to relax and get that happy buzz. I needed to work out how to unwind and cope with the demands of being a new mum, but the only place I knew to turn was in the direction of the bottle. So, I kept on unravelling my already fragile mind with night after night of drinking.

Some of my friends went to the gym, and had smoothies and tea or ran with their buggies, but I could never find the motivation to join them. I could never drag myself out of the dark place I'd drank myself into and see that exercise and cutting out alcohol would have gone a long way towards helping change everything. I couldn't see the light at the end of the tunnel. It was only dark.

66

I had been sold the
idea that drinking
would help me relax.
It was an
extraordinarily
dangerous message.

CHAPTER 3

Escape

Seven-thirty PM, 3rd June 2014

Greenwich, London

The door slams in my face.

I stare at it for a minute before turning around, so my back is pressed against the door my soon-to-be ex-husband has just stormed through. The door we took off its hinges and painted in the perfect shade of Farrow and Ball green. I don't bother opening it. There's no point calling him back or running down the street after him. I slide down the closed door until I'm folded like a crumpled piece of paper on the floor. I sob, heave, and gasp for breath.

Get yourself together.

Get a grip.

This is what you wanted.

Isn't it?

I haul myself up and make my way up the stairs of our renovated Victorian terrace, the worst house on the best street in East London, that we have turned into our home. We've spent years painstakingly demolishing the old and filling it with the new. I run my hand along the banister I spent hours heat-gunning, sanding, and rubbing with wax. All things I had no clue about before we moved into this place.

I try not to look at the faces peering out from behind the glass on the wall, the happy moments I framed and hung along the staircase. My fingers track the places on the walls which nearly crumbled when we took the wallpaper off.

I picture it all falling down around me now.

Peering into Olivia's bedroom I stare at her angelic sleeping face. This perfect little girl who screams the house down every time she wakes up. I swear she gets night terrors because she is inconsolable whenever she wakes up. I don't want to wake her now; I don't want my face to give anything away and worry or upset her. She's already confused about why some of her dad's things are gone and why he isn't here in the mornings anymore.

Before he stormed out I had just told Geoff that I'm taking them away.

I've told him we are no longer going to be living in the house we built, the house that was supposed to be our dream home, the house that was really his dream. Not only is all of that over but we are leaving and moving halfway across the world. I've shattered his dream, and I can't help but feel like I'm the one who is to blame for the destruction of everything we've built. The home, the family, the life, and the future, all ruined because of me. I know that in reality it takes two to tango but right now, after seeing his face so full of anger and being on the receiving end of the furious front door slam, I'm carrying the weight of it all.

I look out of Liv's bedroom window, over the back wall of our garden that borders the park. I stare out at the weathered graves of thousands of soldiers from the Battle of Trafalgar and can't help but envy their eternal slumber. I never sleep now and would swap places with their decaying old bones in a heart beat.

Alfie is sleeping in the next room. I push back the door as quietly as I can to see him breathing heavily on his front, his little bum sticking up in the air inside his baby sleeping bag.

I've spent countless nights on the floor next to his crib with my hand on his back, reassuring him I'm still there. I've tried and failed to creep out without waking him, finally giving in and spending the night scrolling on my phone on the floor. I watch his little back rise and fall as he breathes, sleeping soundly for once.

Outside the back bedroom window, the park is quiet. I will miss this view. Even though it unsettled me slightly the first time I saw it, I've become attached to the gravestones. I have visions of movie scenes being filmed out there, the fog enveloping the graves and skeletal hands smashing through the earth. I'm transported back to a night months ago when I was standing in this exact spot, cradling a newborn Alfie with tears streaming down my face after another argument with Geoff. He's trying to apologise, and I'm sobbing again.

"Just promise you won't leave me alone.

I don't want to do this on my own.

I can't do it alone."

I practically begged him not to leave me when I first suspected he wasn't wholly invested in our life together. He was drifting away from me, spending more and more time at work, and I was losing myself in post-natal depression. The last thing I wanted was to parent our two children alone. I hated the idea of divorce and splitting up a family. I'd lived it as a kid myself and hated the idea of history repeating itself. I didn't want my kids being shunted back and forth between us, but I could see that's where we were headed. I begged him to stay. No matter how hard I tried, I finally accepted I was going to have to walk away, or I would eventually end up being left.

I walk back downstairs, through the kitchen we had created, the beautiful, exposed stock brick walls and marble worktops. I snatch up the bottle of wine I opened in the middle of our argument, the bottle of wine that we usually would have shared but he'd declined before storming out.

My bare feet pad over the slate tiles and through the bifold doors into the garden. I loved creating this space, all flagstones with beds of fragrant roses climbing up the ancient wall that backs onto the park. I breathe in the scent of jasmine filling the late summer night air.

This is everything I thought I wanted but now it's all wrong. It's not my home, it's not somewhere I can stay on my own, I don't want to.

I've made up my mind.

I open my laptop at the outdoor table, pour some more wine, light a cigarette, and start searching for flights to Melbourne. We've talked ourselves in circles trying to work out another way but with the price of houses, childcare, the commuting and working, nannies and juggling everything, it's all too hard. Escaping is the only option that makes sense, to me at least. So, I book the flights and start to scroll through available rentals on the opposite side of the globe.

In the blink of an eye, the house is packed up and sold. Another family will be moving in. I hope it's their dream home and that everything it promises makes them happy in ways it couldn't for us.

The cab is waiting outside, and I watch Geoff say goodbye to the children.

My heart hurts, not metaphorically, it actually aches so much I think it is breaking for real. I feel guilty and ashamed and I can't get out of here fast enough.

"Ok babies, say, 'Bye-bye to Daddy. We will see you in Australia soon, Daddy.' OK, let's go."

I bundle them into the cab, trying not to cry, but the floodgates open as soon as I get in. Alfie looks at me and bursts into tears too.

"Everything ok, miss?" The driver asks.

"Yes, it's ok" I say, and he gives me a sympathetic nod.

We race through Heathrow with the kids scooting along on their bags with wheels, they seem happy enough, distracted by the promise of a journey, an adventure They love the bright lights and the shops at the airport and I want to believe that this whole day and everything that comes after it isn't going to leave them completely traumatised.

With that in mind, I head straight for the lounge.

I set the kids up with iPads and crisps before ordering a large glass of Sav Blanc, if I'm going to be travelling alone with two kids, I should probably do it medicated.

I manage three glasses of wine before we board the plane. I strap the kids into their seats and order a red wine as soon as we are in the air. The hostess parks the drinks trolley behind me, and I openly help myself to more during the flight. No one bats an eyelid, as far as I can see. I don't keep count, but by the time we land in Dubai, I'm in a foggy state somewhere between drunk and already hungover.

Alfie is fast asleep, and Olivia is struggling with her wheelie suitcase down the aisle of the quickly emptying plane. I haul Alfie over my shoulder and try and drag the suitcases with Liv perched on top, my head throbbing.

I burst into tears the second I spot my gorgeous friend Anna waiting for us through the sliding glass doors at arrivals.

"Lex!" She shouts and races over to embrace me.

I feel like I'm going to collapse into her arms. She takes a still-sleeping Alfie from me.

"Hello, my darling godson." She peers at his angelic sleeping face and brushes the hair from his eyes.

I burst into a wave of fresh sobs; she quickly links my arm and points us towards the exit.

"Let's get you out of here."

Back at her place, a gorgeous white townhouse in the middle of an expat complex in media city, we've acclimatised to the sauna-like heat of Dubai and are propped up on sun loungers beside the pool. There's a bottle of Rosé in an ice bucket between us. The kids are racing around with their floaty swimming jackets on, flying up and down the slide and splashing into the water.

This is what I want my life to look like, I think to myself.

Travel, sunshine, wine by the pool,

I've manifested this, and it's here.

I should be happy.

"Right Lex, tell me everything." Anna holds my hand in hers and gives me a concerned look. She knows most of it. We've been best friends since university, and I've talked through it all with her. She's seen our marriage falling apart and knows how I ended up here, but I catch her up on the last bit.

"It was awful," I tell her. "Everyone was crying, I was crying, then Alfie started crying because he saw everyone else crying. I've definitely fucked them all up."

"Darling, you did what you had to do," she reassures me. "They will be happy because you will be happy."

She tops up my glass. I've just inhaled half a bottle of wine, and finally, the alcohol is doing its job of numbing the pain and quietening the incessant noise in my brain.

We drink three bottles by the pool before leaving the kids with Anna's baby girl and their nanny and head out for dinner.

The rest of the night is a blur of laughing, crying and dancing, and I wake at four in the morning with my stomach churning and my head throbbing. I hug the toilet in the guest bathroom and am violently sick before passing out with my head resting on the seat.

The anxiety is back and with the purge over, the voice is back too, telling me how awful I am, how I've messed up everyone's lives, how much the kids will hate me for leaving their father behind, how I am stupid and a failure.

I groan as I move in and out of consciousness and struggle back to the bed to try and get some sleep despite the dreadful spinning and noise in my head.

Anna looks a lot better than I do when I join her on the terrace at breakfast, but she's definitely hungover.

"Lex, I can't keep up with you." She slides her glasses down her nose to look at me. Her eyes are bloodshot and her already porcelain Irish skin is even paler than usual in the blazing sunlight.

"I'm so sorry," I say. "But thank you for last night and for letting us stay; you're the best,"

I try to sound cheerful even though my head throbbing, so I drink my coffee and nibble on a piece of toast.

"We have to be ready for brunch with the others in an hour." Anna groans.

"That will sort us out," I say perkily. "Hair of the dog, darling."

Using alcohol like this was the only way I knew how to deal with the implosion of my life.

I drank to escape the pain, the feelings of shame, and the worries about what the future was going to look like.

I drank because I couldn't face reality, and it's one of the reasons my drinking became such a problem.

For me, grabbing a drink felt like a reflex when anything bad happened or my brain was full of dark thoughts.

It worked in one sense; I didn't have to face any of my feelings head on but the anxiety I felt the next day and the amount I had to drink to drown that feeling out just increased. Alcohol reduced my inhibitions, my judgement, and my memory, so much so that I have a hard time piecing together large parts of the past decade.

Alcohol did what I needed it to do, but I was left completely dependent on it, unable to employ any healthy coping mechanisms when anything went wrong in my life.

I built up such a tolerance to alcohol that I had to drink more and more to get a buzz or any relief from the chatter in my brain. The more alcohol I drank, the worse I felt the next day.

Every time the level of alcohol in my system dropped, my brain went straight into fight or flight. I was constantly anxious and stressed and could only find peace when I managed to get the level of booze in my body just right.

I've spoken to many of my close friends about this period in my life since I quit drinking and asked them if they were ever worried about me. The problem with my problem was that it was hiding in plain sight.

My friends drank with me but didn't realise how much I was drinking on my own. I could hold my alcohol for the most part; I'd built up a tolerance over the years and wouldn't seem drunk until I was at the blackout stage.

I've spoken to Anna about this recently, and she says that she thought it would pass.

"You were going through a rough time," she told me, "so I understood you'd probably be drinking more. It's such a widely accepted form of coping, that it didn't occur to me or anyone else that there could be a real problem."

It was never on them to point it out to me. I knew what I was doing, and the potential trouble I was getting into, but I always thought I could stop if I wanted to—the real issue was that I did not want to.

What I thought I needed in these moments of stress and worry was a quick fix, but what I was trying to fix was a huge problem with my mental state that had been bubbling for years.

If my mental health had been better, I don't believe I would have developed a dependency on alcohol.

If I could turn back the clock, then I would have spent more time and money on working with a therapist and working on myself and less time and money on abusing alcohol, ruining my mental health and my body.

The barrier to changing this was that I didn't believe my need was urgent or worth investing in.

I couldn't see that the problem wasn't the drinking, but the underlying issues.

If I had been in a position to go to rehab, I think I would have been guided to look at the reasons behind why I was drinking and investigate and learn about alternative ways of coping.

I wish I had asked for help before the problem escalated and my drinking threatened to derail my entire life.

Alcohol did what I needed it to do, but I was left completely dependent on it, unable to employ healthy coping mechanisms when anything went wrong

CHAPTER 4

Isolated

Eight AM, 15th December 2020
Greenwich, London

I'm spending Christmas in London, in lockdown, on my own after travelling across the world during a pandemic so the children can be with their father. Now, there's a sentence I never thought I'd say. Geoff's health is deteriorating, and I can't cope. Even though I know this is not about me, I am spiralling. I have lost all sense of perspective and am completely overwhelmed by the idea that we are going to lose him. I can't find the words or the actions to express how I feel about it. It just doesn't make sense. It's not fair, and I can't cope. But it's not about me.

My world collapsed when Geoff called before Christmas to tell me what his medical team had said.

"The doctors have said it's probably best if you come now."

"What do you mean?" I ask, panic rising in my chest. "We can't come, the borders are closed, no one is leaving, and even if we could, they won't let us back in. There are people stranded everywhere; there's no way."

I don't want to go. I know that we should, that the kids need to be with him, and he needs to see them before it's too late, but I'm terrified. What if I get sick? What if one of them gets COVID-19? What if the government won't let us in or out?

What if he dies?

The hugely selfish part of me, who wants to hide under the duvet with a bottle of wine and pretend this isn't happening, doesn't want it to be possible. I don't want to leave Brisbane. I want to stay here and freak out about the pandemic. I can't handle adding in a last trip to see Geoff, a last time for the kids, a last Christmas, a last goodbye. I can't do it. I want someone else to be the adult here.

From the relative safety of Australia, the UK looks like COVID hell. Boris Johnson is merrily condemning the elderly to their deaths and prattling on about herd immunity. My friends are taking it all in their stride; what other choice do they have? I know it's awful of me not to want to go. I know that none of this would have happened if I hadn't moved the kids away in the first place. I know. I wish none of it had ever happened; not his cancer, not our divorce, not the children and I living somewhere else, not the pandemic and not us on a deserted flight with masks and face shields on. Wishing all that away, though, means the future I've been blessed with, the one where I live in Australia with the kids and I get to marry my wonderful fiancé Warren... that's all gone.

Warren is struggling to cope with my mood swings. One minute, I'm manic, and the next, I'm angry, and in both instances, I'm usually drunk or hungover. No matter how hard he tries, there's no way for him to help me. He wants to keep us safe and doesn't want us to travel to London, but he knows we must.

We are granted an exemption and head off through the empty airports. Some of the other travellers are sporting full hazmat suits. We try our best to keep our distance from everyone, which isn't hard on our plane from Brisbane, which has 12 passengers.

I stay with friends for the first few weeks while we make sure the kids and I haven't picked up COVID-19 on the flights over. We take tests in the cold car parks of football stadiums and shopping centres and receive text messages a few hours later saying we are negative. The kids head off to spend time with Geoff, and my heart breaks for them all. I feel entirely alone with Warren on the other side of the world and Alfie and Olivia with their dad. I can't help but feel like I've brought this on myself. My choices have brought me here, and while the pandemic has forced us into isolation, I feel like every decision I've made has brought me to this place where I am cut off from everyone and everything I've ever loved.

I'm not good when I'm left to my own devices. On my own, I drink, wallow, and watch crappy TV all night, then sleep all day. That's the cycle I fall into for weeks on end. The days resemble Groundhog Day. We aren't booked on a flight home until the end of January, and I can't even begin to contemplate how I will cope with two weeks in quarantine if we make it back to Australia.

"I just hate being here; I hate it so much. It's cold and miserable, and Boris is a fucking idiot."

"I know; I hate that you're there too, not long now, though." Warren is trying to be positive, but I know he is as stressed as I am about the possibility of us getting sick or stuck here.

"Boris is not doing anything right; he's just so stupid. At least he's not closed the borders yet, which is ridiculous, obviously, but good news for us, I guess. Someone posted in that stranded Aussies Facebook group that they've been bumped off their last three flights. A family with little kids. They reckon the only way to guarantee a seat is to be in business." I'm rambling and stressing myself out after a whole night of doom-scrolling.

"Look, I'm going to see if I can change your return tickets to business class, so at least you've got a better chance of making it on."

"Really? Babe, that would be amazing." My heart swells. I feel so guilty for putting him through this, but I know it will make him feel better to do something to help. If there's a problem, he will be the one to find the solution. I down the last of my gin and breathe a sigh of relief. I wander through to the kitchen to pour another drink. "What would I do without you? I know this is horrible for you, too, and I know how worried you must be. I'm sorry."

"Don't worry, it's ok. We've got this. I love you."

"Love you more."

I scroll through my emails and spot an invitation to an online yoga class with a difference, a very appealing difference. 'Gin Yoga' is about to start, and I'm delighted to join in.

Our instructor, Simon, appears on my screen, sitting cross-legged in a candlelit room with a bottle of gin and a full fishbowl glass in front of him.

"Welcome, namaste, and cheers everyone."

It's the weirdest thing, but I'm here for it and join him in swigging as much gin as possible after every sun salutation. I'm drunk, but that's par for the course. I stay drunk by drinking the remainder of the gin and wine in the house when the class is over. I go online and order ready-made cocktails from Lockdown Liquor and pass out.

I lose track of the days again. They all blend into one another, only punctuated by wandering through Greenwich Park in the cold. I walk around the grounds, which are always scattered with people avoiding each other. The rose bushes are bare, the ground is frosty, and my breath creates puffs of smoke as I force myself up and down the hills. I've been binge-watching Bridgerton on Netflix and find a little joy in snapping photos of the house where it was filmed and sharing them on my Instagram.

By the time Christmas Eve comes around, I'm still on a drinking binge, but my body has decided to attempt to bring that to an end. The universe delivers a dose of schadenfreude, and I spend the night throwing up, hugging the toilet, and trying to convince myself I've got food poisoning instead of alcohol poisoning. The timing couldn't be worse; I'm supposed to spend Christmas Day with the kids at Geoff's house. Even though I know it's not COVID, my entire body feels like it's shutting down. I'm shaking and can barely make it down the stairs. My legs buckle, and I slide down the last few steps on my bum. I try to keep some coffee down before making the dreaded phone call.

"I'm so sorry baby, I can't come today. I'm sick and can't be near Daddy if I've caught something. I will see you in a couple of days."

"But Mum," Alfie says, struggling to hide that he's upset, "we had the whole day planned; we even set you a seat at the table." I'm devastated not to see the kids on Christmas Day, but selfishly, I'm ok with not spending a whole day with Geoff, his new wife (they got married a week ago) and his first wife. All three of us with him and all his kids is a lot. It would be nice in a Modern Family way to do the whole together thing, especially as it might be the only chance we get, but the decision has been taken out of my hands. I've isolated myself with my drinking, and I can't help but think I'm exactly where I deserve to be: alone.

The next few days go by in a blur of sleeping, shaking, retching, going from hot to cold, and then trying to drink again. I ease back into keeping liquids down by getting back on my Baileys coffee and working up the strength to go out for a walk. I wander down to the testing site at the Old Royal Naval College in the centre of town to ensure I'm not carrying around a weird COVID strain. The beautiful old building is where Geoff and I got married ten years ago, and it always makes me feel a little sad that everything was so beautiful in the beginning and then turned to shit.

There's no queue at the testing tent, and I wander inside after giving my details to the man sitting behind Perspex at the entrance. I'm handed the kit and instructed to swab myself.

"You have to do it deeper than that," the nurse, standing just outside the little bay I'm in, says unhelpfully.

Who wants to jab the swab further up their nostril? I tried to do it again, and she seemed satisfied. I seal it all up and pass it to the guy behind the screen on my way out of the tent. It reminds me of the place you'd expect to see in a disaster zone. I guess this is a disaster, the whole world stopping, waiting to see how many of us will die, who'll get sick, who won't, who will get it right, who will fuck it up completely.

My anxiety is next level as I walk through the streets after leaving the testing site, dodging other people, crossing the road if I spot someone coming towards me without a mask.

I stop at the supermarket on the way back from the testing site and pull my mask up when I see a couple without them. God, I hate this. I grab three bottles of red wine, a pack of mince pies, gin, and tonic water.

"Is that all?" The cashier asks, eyeing my selection.

"20 Marlboro lights, please."

He slides the pack under the plastic partition; I tap my card, grab my supplies, and head back out into the dark street.

Despite the lockdown, plenty of people are out, and I don't want to be near them, so I shuffle quickly back down the side streets to my temporary home. It's a tiny terrace near the pub where they filmed *Only Fools and Horses*, just a few streets back from the river Thames and around the corner from the Cutty Sark. If the world were a different place right now it would be a great spot to explore London from, but tonight it feels lonely and claustrophobic all at the same time.

I've got a front-row seat to the soap opera lives of the people on both sides of the street, a crying baby in the house on the left, and teenagers banging up and down the stairs on the right. I can hear their conversations, arguments, laughter, and even what they're watching on TV. I know we watch the Covid updates simultaneously as we tune into the news every night. I feel a pang of jealousy when I see the familiar news readers sitting behind the desk from which I used to read the headlines. Going to work right now would be dreadful, but reporting on a huge, earth-changing story like this is why I used to love doing it.

I turn on all the fairy lights the owners have strung around the lounge and put on the tiny Christmas tree lights. I plop down on the sofa, flick through different channels on the TV and start scrolling on my phone. I'm two bottles of wine in and feeling distraught when I see Warren is awake and online on the other side of the world. I call to catch him before he starts work.

"We have to get out of here," I'm crying down the phone after only a few pleasantries.

I know there's nothing he can do, but he's the only one I can drunkenly vent to. My friends are all stuck trying to home-school their kids. Most of them are sick or have been ill because COVID is spreading all over the place.

"I wish you were home too, not long now, baby."

Warren has been sending me funny gifts in the post to cheer me up and has upgraded our flights, spending thousands of dollars to ensure we can get home.

"I'm sorry, I know. I'll try to hold it together. I'll be ok. Don't worry, honestly," I lie.

I spend New Year's Eve drinking and watching movies. I run through every episode of *Sex in the City*, then rewatch *Bridget Jones*. When it gets close to midnight, I head outside into the back garden with a glass of bubbles to toast the end of the crappiest year ever. The neighbours are out and pass me a sparkler over the fence.

"Happy New Year."

We smiled through the fence panels at each other, and then all looked up as fireworks as a drone show fills the sky.

Later I lay in bed staring at the ceiling and listening to fireworks. I think about how much I miss the kids and I wish they were with me instead of their dad.

Geoff arrives at the Airbnb a week later to drop off the children. I try to hide my shock when I see him looking so old and tired. His skin is grey, and his eyes are sunken. He struggles to walk even a short distance and sits down as soon as he makes it inside. I hesitate before kissing him on the cheek, and I can sense the kids watching.

We talk about what the kids got from Santa and what games they've been playing to pass the time. Then it's time to say goodbye. They look so tiny, trying to hold back tears while visibly distressed. There's nothing I can say to make it better. I feel the shame and guilt course through my body, and I burst into tears as I push the door closed behind him. The kids and I curl up on the sofa, sobbing and holding each other.

The following day, we catch a cab to the hotel at the airport, and I down two Valiums trying to stave off a panic attack. We take Covid tests and are told to wait for the results to see if they'll let us check-in.

In the middle of the night, three of us sleeping in the same bed, I get a text saying Alfie's test was inconclusive and he has to do it again, so I have to wake him up and get him to fill another tube with spit.

"I can't make any spit," he tells me.

How do you explain how to spit? I wonder. After a quick google search, I put him in the bath and give him a big glass of water. Relaxed and hydrated he manages to fill the tube. It's so gross.

We are all miserable, tired and grumpy, the next morning and just an hour before check-in, we get the all-clear.

We haven't been bumped from our flight and are finally going home.

The kids smile for the first time when we realise the plane is practically empty, and they can't believe they are sitting in business class with flat beds.

They fall asleep quickly, and I drink champagne and then move to red wine until I pass out.

"Stand on the spot there and spread your legs and arms." A guy dressed in Army uniform barks.

It's not the welcome home we were expecting, and I'm in tears in front of some very stern-looking army guys.

The soldiers run things at Brisbane Airport and separate us to let the dogs sniff for COVID-19.

We are ushered into lines and told to get on buses before we are given the name of the quarantine hotel to which we are allocated. We end up one hour south of our home on the Gold Coast.

I pass the two weeks by drinking, doing yoga, eating crap food, getting deliveries from friends, watching the kids playing the Nintendo, and endless YouTube.

We have a view of the sunny outside, I opted for adjoining rooms rather than an ocean view. I can't hear the ocean but the space of two rooms is making life in quarantine a little more bearable. Warren visits, and we get to wave at him from our window ten floors up as he stands across the street. Our only real human interaction is through our daily COVID tests from nurses who arrive at our door with army escorts.

After 14 days, we are released.

Geoff dies nine months later.

He had a seizure and was taken to hospital, where they put him in a coma. He was confused when he was brought around and asked for the kids. I considered returning them to England, but I couldn't wrap my head around the idea that he might be gone before we landed. Or that their last memory of him would be of him in a hospital bed, not able to work out who they were.

So, we told him we loved him over FaceTime when he was lucid, and I wrestled with feeling like I had destroyed everyone's lives.

I received a text saying he'd died while I was sitting on the side of the local pool watching the kids in their swimming lessons. I struggled to hide my tears behind my sunglasses and couldn't bring myself to tell Alfie and Olivia until we got home. I'll never shake the image of their faces when I tell them.

"Darlings, I'm so sorry, but Daddy has died."

They looked at each other and dissolved into floods of tears. There was nothing I could do or say to make it better. We spent the next two days in bed together. I carried on day-drinking and crying, trying to make it through each awful hour.

The drinking didn't stop when they went back to school.

If anything, it escalated.

I was consumed by grief for them and for the future without their dad, as well as a future where I was their only parent. I was bloated, sluggish, anxious, and depressed. I was constantly getting into silly arguments with Warren and I was more impatient than ever with the kids. None of them deserved it, but I couldn't shake myself out of the low I'd sunk to.

The rut I'd found myself in was hardly surprising.

I could see no reason to stop drinking and didn't want to face all the thoughts and feelings that surfaced when I was sober. I knew I needed to talk about Geoff's death, so I went back to my therapist, but we didn't touch on my drinking. She didn't ask, and I didn't tell. I was still in denial about it being a problem.

66

I could see no reason to stop drinking and didn't want to face all the thoughts and feelings that surfaced when I was sober

CHAPTER 5

Break

Four-thirty pm, 12th October 2021

Brisbane

12 Days Sober

"I'm doing this," I say to myself. "I'm not even thinking about drinking, but now I am thinking about drinking. I'm not, nope not me, damn it, I am." I shake my head with disappointment.

"Mum, when's dinner?" Alfie shouts from the other room where he's in the middle of some video game shooting things and shouting at his friends through his headset. I'm supposed to be making dinner, but I keep walking around in circles, going from one task to another, and can't focus on anything. First, I'm folding laundry, then I realise there's still a load of clothes in the washing machine that need to go on the line. I think they've been there since yesterday.

I wander upstairs aimlessly and pick up a coffee cup then wander back downstairs. I attempt to put it in the full dishwasher, realising I haven't emptied it since breakfast. I think about getting the kids to help me, then dismiss the idea as too hard and start doing it myself. I can't deal with the arguments today. Then I remember I meant to be working out what they're going to eat for dinner. My chest tightens, my fists clench, and I grit my teeth. God, I want a glass of wine.

I stopped drinking 12 days ago.

12 days, 4 hours, 32 minutes and seven seconds ago, according to my sober app.

I'm keeping track of the next 75 days on my first proper break from alcohol in quite some time. This challenge is a good way of not making it all about drinking, even though it really is for me. I have to work out twice a day, drink loads of water, eat healthily, and not drink any alcohol. I would normally have had a glass by now, of course—more than one, if I were honest.

This is the cycle I'm trying to break, to see if I can stop drinking, and become a better version of myself. Can I function without alcohol and eventually stop thinking about it, or am I so far gone that I need to get my arse to rehab?

No. I can do this. I've got this.

Warren is on board too with the 75 days of health. We've joined a group of friends all supporting each other through texts, group chats and Instagram messages. There's a flurry every night as we all post our daily progress pictures along with snaps of the books we are reading or the new place we've found to walk.

No one else seems to be struggling quite like me with the no-drinking part, so I'm refraining from telling them all just how hard it is for now.

I want to do this and have a real break from booze.

I'm trying to focus on the fact that I also want to look and feel better for our wedding. We've rescheduled it for February 2022, and even though I'm nervous about admitting it, I really don't want to drink anymore. The fog of the past god knows how long is finally lifting. I feel like I'm waking up from the permanent hangover that was my life, and I'm actually seeing the light at the end of the tunnel.

"But you're going to drink at your wedding, aren't you?" My friend Jess is concerned when she sees me holding a glass of sparkling water that Saturday.

I get it, I would have asked this question before, and despite my positivity, I feel my determination wobble. Then, I impulsively bite the bullet and say it out loud.

"Nope, I don't think so. I reckon I'm done with it. I honestly don't think I want to drink ever again."

Her face is an absolute picture.

She lights another cigarette and skulls the remainder of her champagne.

"Seriously? Why? Do you think you're an alcoholic or something?"

"Well, yes. I do."

I've never said that out loud and I'm not totally sure I believe it. I know that I drink too much. I definitely drink way more than any health professional would recommend, but am I an alcoholic?

Probably.

I can tell Jess is weighing this up.

If I think I'm an alcoholic and she drinks as much as I do, then is she one too? Yes, she drinks like I did when we are out, but she probably stops when she goes home. I don't think she is like me. I've been drinking on my own and blacking out every night. But I'm not about to start laying it out and making distinctions.

She's several glasses of champagne in on a sunny Spring Saturday morning. We are at a mutual friend's house overlooking the Brisbane River and everyone is milling around drinking at 11 am. It's only now that I'm not drinking that it starts to look a little odd.

I mean, I look odd because I'm not gearing up to dance on the tables, but they look odd too.

Why are they all drinking the day away?

Does it matter?

Why do I care?

They're all going to be wasted before the sun goes down, and slurring their words and getting into stupid arguments. It's the same as it has always been but now, I am looking at everyone from behind my shades and trying to work out which ones have the same problem as me—the inability to say no to a drink and then to stop drinking after starting. It's like I've been walking around with actual booze goggles on and now I've taken them off, I'm starting to get my eyesight back. The haze is clearing and I'm looking at it from a totally different place.

I make my excuses to a couple of people an hour or so later and tell Warren I'll see him at home, then I quietly leave early.

It's something I would normally have never done. I'd normally be one of the last ones standing, losing track of time and stumbling home. Luckily, Warren gets it. He can sense my unease and only stays when I urge him to.

An hour later, I received a text, a drunken, angry text.

"You could have said goodbye," it reads.

It's my friend Sasha, or the person I thought was my friend. She's stirring. I know she's talking behind my back with Jess and anyone else who will listen about me not drinking, and she is about to go full-blown bitch on me. Part of me wants to tell her to go and fuck herself but the people-pleasing side of me wins.

"Sorry, you were in the middle of dancing, and I had to dash. See you at the school Mum's lunch."

No reply.

I'm not surprised, but I watch the phone and hope to see the little dots appear, telling me I was wrong about her being a complete cow about this.

But no, nothing.

Whatever.

I tell Warren when he comes home. He's sober, too, but he's used to skipping the alcohol at events like that. He has that superpower I lack, the ability to go without alcohol and be sociable. But he sees how upset I am and hugs me.

"You don't need them." He's doing his best to reassure me, but I can tell he's worried about the fallout. He has been friends with this bunch for longer than I have, and it could become awkward if this really does dissolve our friendship.

That night, I toss and turn, trying to ignore the horrible voices in my head. Drinking would have drowned them out, but now they're all I can hear.

I brought this onto myself

Why am I such a loser?

Why can't I just drink like everyone else?

Why does it always have to be so dramatic?

My friends all think I'm boring now.

I am boring now.

I have spent the past three years hanging out with the same group of girls. All Mums with kids around the same age as mine, all drinkers, *big* drinkers, who love a long lunch, a brunch, a weekend BBQ, a trip to a pub, winery, club—you get the picture. Girls like me, or girls like the old me. Girls whose social life revolves around drinking. Like me, but not like me now

Now I've stopped, for good.

I hope.

We have always encouraged each other to drink. It's how we have fun. There would be a bunch of us all ordering expensive bottles of champagne, ordering waiters to deliver the bottles with the sparkler in the top, downing shots called things like, *Wet Pussy's* and *Cock Sucking Cowboys*, being the loudest in the bar, the centre of attention.

Some of that attention was positive. We made friends easily, other girls would laugh, some would join the party. But now, more and more I've seen the pity, the side eye, the whispers. The 20-somethings watching this bunch of designer hand bag-toting women who should know better. 40-something mums, falling over, falling out of bars and taxis, shouting at doormen. I've seen the judging, and I get it; it's not a good look, and now I'm not drinking, I can't unsee it.

Even though I can tell that these friendships are heading for the dumpster, I give it one last shot in the hope that I don't have to cut myself off entirely.

When I arrive at Jess's house after school drop-off with a bottle of non-alcoholic bubbles in my hand, I find them all drinking the real stuff already.

It's 9:30 am and while this has never bothered me before—in fact, I normally would have been the one opening the first bottle—it strikes me as marginally terrifying. I know how quickly these girls can get drunk, especially considering none of them have eaten much more than a carrot stick since 2019.

This is going to get messy.

I can feel their eyes on me as I open my bottle and offer them some, already knowing they're going to decline.

I have a sinking feeling; the mean girls are in full effect and it's Wednesday and I'm not wearing pink. I honestly feel like I'm in that teen movie, I'm in the firing line because I've made them feel uncomfortable, I'm no longer towing the line, following suit by drinking and cackling and making a show. I stand out and I'm drawing attention to myself, and they don't like it, not one little bit.

We get in a cab and Sasha looks me up and down.

"Still not drinking then? This is probably going to be pretty boring for you."

It's not a question.

She's made up her mind and doesn't think there's any point in me being there.

I'm starting to think the same.

"No, I'm good thanks, I've got stuff to do with the kids later anyway so ...," I trail off lamely.

There's an auction at the lunch and my friends are so loud that they keep getting yelled at by the auctioneer. I probably wouldn't have taken much notice before but now I'm mortified.

I'm embarrassed to be with them.

As I sip my mocktail the other women in the restaurant are throwing them daggers and I want to die. I've spent so much time and effort making myself believe I've found people I can hang out with, and now I can see clearly that we have nothing in common.

"Girls, I have to go."

"What, aren't you coming to the bar with us? You can't leave."

They chime in with fake sweetness, asking me to stay, but I'm on the verge of tears, and I don't think I can take any more of the mean girl shit. They've been taking photos and excluding me all day, which I shouldn't care about as it's completely pathetic, but I do care.

I care that I feel out of place, exposed and stupid all at once.

I know that I'm being sensitive and that everything feels weird because I'm sober, but I also don't need to put up with the shitty way they're treating me and everyone around them anymore. So, I make my excuses and rush outside to find a cab. I manage to hold back the tears until I get out of sight. I jump into a cab, mumble my address, and bury my face in my hands, wiping running mascara away and trying to shake the thoughts of how much a drink would help me feel better.

My head and heart are a complete jumble. It's like I'm seeing everything clearly, but I can't quite make complete sense of it all. Every feeling I have is amplified and exaggerated and confusing all at once and I don't know where to start.

I want to make a clear break from booze, but my entire life revolves around it.

My friends and drinking are inextricably linked. Everything I do is soaked in booze, it has a sheen from all the alcohol it has been doused in. Taking a step back, I can see how easily it can go up in flames. Without the alcohol, it just doesn't make sense. I know that I need to break up with these so-called friends to help break the cycle of drinking I'm in, but I'm scared of not having girlfriends around when I'm trying to change so much.

I try and focus on the good stuff, it's now over three weeks since I last had a drink.

22 days, 11 hours, 9 minutes and 48 seconds, to be precise.

I can't stop checking my app to see how close I am getting to the 75 days. I know if I can make it there, I can stop for good, but it seems very far away, and the wine is really calling me today.

I pull myself together, wipe the makeup off my face, change out of my dress into some active wear, scrape my hair back, grab the dog's leads and usher them out the front door and down the hill to pick up the kids from school.

I want to be here for them, I think to myself as I wander down the hill feeling the breeze racing up to meet us and start listing the reasons why I'm doing this and what stopping drinking will mean.

I don't want to still be in a bar wasting money and losing track of time, begging my mum to pick them up and then rolling in wasted to see her disapproving face.

I don't want to wake up with a hangover every single day.

I want to be here for the kids, properly be here.

I want to be able to pick them up from school - to walk down this hill and underneath the blossoming jacaranda trees with the dogs, take it all in, and hear about Olivia and Alfie's day.

I want to embrace the fact that it's a privilege that I get to do this.

I want to be present on my wedding day and start my marriage with Warren with the clear intention of not fucking it up like I did the last one.

I repeat all of this over and over to myself until I see the kids smiling and running across the school field to meet me.

This is what I want.

When we are home, and the kids have reluctantly settled down to do some homework, I pick up one of the books from the stack I've been reading on the coffee table. I've been trying to embrace everything about giving up alcohol. It's part of this challenge that we read ten pages of a non-fiction book every day. As a journalist and an English Literature graduate, I used to spend an awful lot of time reading, but recently it's fallen by the wayside. Blacking out in bed every night doesn't exactly lend itself to reading much more than what's on my phone, and hangovers aren't normally ideal reading buddies either.

The books at the top of the pile are *This Naked Mind* and *Quit Like A Woman*, and reading them makes me feel like I'm using my brain for the first time in forever. I'm engaged and invested in learning everything about what is happening to me now I've stopped drinking and reading is helping me find new reasons to stick with it.

As my eyes move back and forth across the words, taking them all in, I find myself breathing a sigh of relief. My foggy brain, my fluctuating emotions, my crying, questioning myself, feeling out of place, thinking about alcohol all the time - it's all normal. At this stage of my recovery, what I'm experiencing is par for the course. I'm still getting used to the terminology, I play with the words and try to work out how I feel about them.

I'm in recovery.

It's all going to take a little getting used to. I have convinced myself for such a long time that I didn't have a problem and that I didn't drink too much.

I wasn't an alcoholic.

I didn't abuse alcohol.

I drank like everyone else.

I didn't need to give up.

But I am, and I did, and now, I'm going through it all, I'm detoxing and dealing with the cravings, and I need to go through it to get to the other side.

It's going to be worth it.

I can do this.

I decide to listen to the cravings and give them what they really want, sugar.

I've read about how much sugar I've been ingesting through alcohol, and even though I always knew that wine was empty calories, I hadn't realised how much I would be craving sweet stuff to replace it.

I head for the pantry and grab a bag of lolly snakes; rip open the bag and start chomping through them. I mix up a fake gin and tonic and pick up my phone. Now, I think it's time to implement some more advice I've picked up along the road to recovery.

It's time to start sharing some of this stuff and find my new tribe.

I search for sober influencers, non-alcoholic drink brands, and inspirational accounts and follow them all, then I start unfollowing all the pubs, clubs, restaurants, and people who post nothing but drinking pics on their feeds – including Jess and Sasha. I block them so they can't play any part in the next chapter of my life. I know this is going to cause trouble, but this is for my mental health. I need to stop scrolling and seeing all things alcohol, drinking, and drunk related and I need to cut out the toxic people in my life. I snap a picture of my non-alcoholic gin and tonic, and post it to my story and write, #alcoholfree, and cheers myself.

I can do this.

"

This is the cycle I'm trying to break. Can I function without alcohol and eventually stop thinking about it?

CHAPTER 6

Detox

Five-Twenty-Five AM, 15th May 2004

Leicester Square, London

I grab my bag and phone and cram in the rest of my belongings, which are strewn all over the back seat, as I stumble out of the car and make a beeline for the corner shop. Hovering somewhere between still drunk and already very hungover, I grab two Red Bulls and some mints and ask the guy behind the counter for 20 Marlboro lights. He gives me a nod. He's seen me carry out this ritual every Saturday and Sunday morning for the past year and is probably wondering how I'm still alive.

"Cheers," I say as I grab my supplies and head for the steps of a nearby doorway. Leicester Square is always busy with people heading on to another club or home from a night out, no matter what time of day, so my dishevelled appearance doesn't draw much concern or attention.

The ground is damp, but I don't have the energy or wherewithal to stop and work out if it's from rain or someone's piss before I plonk myself down and crack open my can of caffeine and light a fag. The combination of the vodka Red Bulls I ingested in the club I stumbled out of about an hour ago in Clapham and the straight Red Bull I'm now layering on top makes my stomach churn. I will need some real coffee and food to make it through the morning without puking or falling asleep.

My hands shake as I rapidly drag on my cigarette and exhale smoke into the dewy morning air. I swig my drink and rub under my eyes to remove the inevitable mascara smudges, trying to pull myself together enough to walk into work. I meant to be reading the 6 o'clock bulletin on the radio in 30 minutes, but I haven't even started writing it or working out the top story. My colleague Bec will already be there, head down, typing away and sending scripts to the network for me.

It's meant to be my job; I'm meant to edit the scripts for the whole network of radio stations and newsreaders across the country, but recently, things have been falling apart. When I say things, of course, I mean me.

Bec has noticed. She has seen me stumbling in straight from more than one night out, only to fall asleep on the studio sofa. She has seen me chain-smoking through my break. She has even seen me leave cash hanging out of an ATM and walk away without realising it. She's been noticing my mistakes before I send them out and has been picking up the slack.

I don't know how to thank her or tell her that I know I'm being completely shit. The problem is I don't want to acknowledge it because that would mean that there really is a problem, and the problem is me and my drinking, so I just mumble, "Sorry," as I fling my bag on my desk and log in hurriedly. She has her headphones on and looks up only briefly before looking back down again and carrying on working.

The next six hours go by in a blur, I read the bulletins on XFM with Jimmy Carr hosting the show. He is on form and way too quick-witted for me today. I read the news, and he interrupts halfway through the final story with a joke. Instead of some banter, which I imagine he was hoping for, I giggle and finish the bulletin.

"That's the latest on XFM, I'm Alex Hyndman."

I can feel my face turning redder by the second, the heat creeping up my chest and onto my cheeks. I'm mortified. I need a drink.

As soon as midday rolls around, that's exactly what I get. I drag two of the producers to the pub and order flaming sambucas and gin and tonics in glasses the size of goldfish bowls. We settle in for the afternoon and take turns going to the bar. When they start complaining about needing to head home, I call them lightweights and start scrolling through my phone, messaging everyone to see who's out and where. I score an invite to my friend Kate's house in Camden. Off I trot to the tube, chain-smoking as I go, my handbag clinking on my hip with the two gin glasses I've stolen in it.

I can only picture the rest of the day as snippets. Some of it is slow motion, some I see from above like I'm dead and looking down on another version of me. I see other parts of the day and then night like Polaroid pictures stuck in a photo album that I'm flicking through.

There's me on the tube with my head lolling around.

Me in a taxi after I miss my stop.

Me lying on the grass outside Kate's flat, laughing after falling over.

Me in a mini cab with a driver trying to work out my address.

Me inviting people to my flat on the King's Road, the one owned by one of my Uni friends.

Me spilling red wine all over her brand-new white carpets.

Me filling an ashtray on the windowsill and leaving it overflowing.

Me helping myself to her mini bottles of champagne in the fridge.

Me stumbling up and down the stairs to let more friends in and buy more cheap off-licence wine.

Me agreeing that one of my friends can kick in the door to the flat because I've locked the keys inside and he needs to get his house keys to go home.

Then it's morning.

I see my wretched, sad self, waking up to the sight of the door off its hinges, the sound of the horn blaring from my work driver outside and the vision of my phone with thirty-two missed calls on it.

This is the kind of night that makes me sick with shame.

It's the kind of behaviour I don't want to admit to, the kind of thing I know I should be completely mortified by and I am.

I hate the fact that I drank so much that I put myself in all kinds of dangerous situations. I don't know exactly how I managed to survive this period of binge-drinking and risk-taking unscathed.

I remember trying to laugh it all off, the drinking, the lateness, the unhinged antics, all of it. I don't know what part I thought was funny, but somehow I convinced myself I was having fun.

The truth of it is that I alienated myself from many work colleagues, missed opportunities, and I lost a lot of friends – including my poor University friend who let me share her flat. It is all so hard to admit to and it is memories of nights like this that I know I've been trying to forget by continuing to drink.

Now that the booze is leaving my system, all these memories are flooding back. They're keeping me awake at night and I'm having the most vivid dreams. I see the faces of the people I pissed off, the ones I treated like shit, the ones who saw me at my lowest. I watch myself kiss faceless guys in clubs and wake up next to people I hardly know. I see the potentially horrific and awful situations I could have ended up in. I see myself getting attacked, hit by cars, and falling down stairs. I constantly wake up in a cold sweat with soaking wet sheets. I look around the room frantically, convinced I'm back in London and that I've fallen asleep on the tube or in the office under a desk, before I realise I'm home.

"Are you ok, babe?" Warren is not accustomed to my fitful sleep; I used to sleep like the dead.

"Yeah, it's okay." I exhale, picking up my phone to check the time—2 am.

"I just keep having these awful dreams that are more like flash-backs," I try to explain. "I'm reliving these awful moments, and it feels like my brain is punishing me, you know. It's like I'm torturing myself."

"You are doing so well; it's bound to be weird for a while, but it will disappear." He's groggy but always wise. "Didn't one of your books say that visions and weird dreams were normal?" he asks, already knowing the answer,.

"I know, yeah, it's normal I get it, but it's like my brain is trying to make me relive some of the most awful things I've done, and I really do not need to remember. It's like my mind is begging me to stay sober, the devil on my shoulder has been pushed aside, and the angel is trying to get me to listen and stick to this."

"You've got this honey." He rolls over and starts snoring.

I keep staring into the dark, trying to make sense of it all, and finally give up on sleep. I scroll through my phone, reading articles about getting sober and attempt to learn more about this stage of my sobriety, my so-called recovery journey. The shakes, the naps, the vivid dreams, the endless sugar cravings and the urge to hide from everyone is all apparently normal. I haven't had a drink in 6 weeks. I'm over halfway to the 75-day goal, and I know that I must keep going; I'm on board with what the angel on my shoulder is telling me and I'm trying to say it out loud as often as I can.

On the rare occasion I do go out and socialise, I order mocktails and talk about my decision not to drink to make myself believe as much as to have something to talk about. I figure that if I say it out loud enough, it will be harder to go back on.

"Will you just have a few drinks when you're done with the 75 days?" A friend asks. I pretend to consider it, but I know the answer has to be no.

I'm gradually convincing myself that I will do everything in my power to stick to this way of life and never, ever go back. But occasionally, I think, *what if?*

What if I just had a drink?

No one would ever know.

I need help.

I've come this far on adrenaline, the feeling of something new, the novelty of trying and succeeding. But I can see people on my challenge already going back to their old ways, and even though that might be ok for them, I know it's very dangerous territory for me.

I must keep away from boozy people and boozy places for now. Maybe I'll be able to go back in small doses soon, but for now, I can't face being surrounded by people who drink; I need to find people in real life who don't.

"Hi, I'm Alex, and I'm an alcoholic."

"I haven't had a drink for 45 days and ... um ... I came here to find people like me I guess ..."

I bite the inside of my cheek hard to try and stop the tears.

"I used to drink a lot, and I scared my kids when I got drunk. Then their dad died, so I stopped drinking to be there for them ..."

That's it. That's all I can say before I burst into tears. Huge sobs escape from my body despite my best efforts to catch my breath, I'm shuddering and bawling.

This is my first AA meeting, and I've definitely made an impression.

We are in a park in East Brisbane, it's a boiling hot November day, and the sun is beating down on us at 11 am. We are in a circle under a tree; plastic chairs that were chained to the trunk have been placed around it, and a group of 12 of us are seated in them, all facing each other. Most are making eye contact and smiling at me as I try to regain my composure. No one is jumping in or trying to calm me down. They're just letting me have my moment, and I feel vulnerable, seen, exposed and sad, all at the same time.

How did I end up here?

I'm angry at myself because this was a long time coming. The writing was on the wall, as they say, but there's still part of me that can't quite believe I'm an alcoholic at an AA meeting. I'm spilling my guts to strangers. Luckily, they are strangers who get it, strangers who have probably all had it a lot worse than I have. I scrub my sparkly silver sandals around in the deep brown dusty earth and wring my hands as I try to tell my story without completely losing it.

I make it through the rest, telling them in detail about what happened the night I fell down the stairs in front of my kids, how I've been struggling with friends who still drink and finding a place where I feel like I can explore this new sober me.

They all smile at me warmly and then the next person starts their turn. Everyone is open, and they all manage to hold it together a lot better than me.

A couple are travelling around Australia and have stopped in at the meeting with their dog, a little Cavalier King Charles who I'm dying to cuddle. There's a guy who's a chef who has burnt his foot and hobbled into the meeting before explaining in gruesome detail about the incident with the chip fryer. There are a couple of much older guys who could be in their eighties. A woman who looks around my age with dyed pink hair and lots of facial piercings, and the woman hosting the meeting. Janice looks like she's heading for work in a bank. She's dressed super conservatively with a polished bob.

When it's Janice's turn, she talks about how she's gone from being homeless and depending on the Salvation Army for a place to sleep and something to eat, to being able to volunteer there and help others like her. She's been sober for 7 years and now runs this group and two others.

I know that alcoholics aren't the dishevelled old man on the park bench with a bottle of whisky in a brown paper bag, I understand that, but to actually see the evidence in front of me is the affirmation I needed for today. It's the reinforcement I need to keep going and accept that this is who I am. Whether or not I believe it's a disease that I've succumbed to because of a genetic pre-disposition to addiction, or whether

I believe it's the choices I've made to drink and abuse alcohol, it doesn't make a difference.

I am like these people, and they are like me, we all have a common enemy: booze. It doesn't matter how or why it got hold of us. What matters is that we don't let it get in again, and we never go back.

At the end of the meeting, Janice asks Tash, the one with pink hair, to say the serenity prayer. Everyone else chimes in, but I don't know it, although I recognise it perhaps from a movie.

God, grant me the serenity

To accept the things I cannot change;

Courage to change the things I can;

And wisdom to know the difference.

Grant me serenity … well, that bit is worth praying for.

I'm looking for calm in my life after so many years of turmoil. I close my eyes and say *Amen* with them, then stand up to help start packing up the chairs. I slide them on top of each other so they can rest against the tree, and wait for the next group of people whose lives have been upended by drinking to come and seek serenity.

Janice, Tash, and James, the chef, all come over to me as I'm putting a chair on top of the stack.

"Thank you for sharing that today," Janice says as she holds out a dog-eared, well-thumbed little blue book.

"I only have this one with me, but I can bring you a new one next week."

I look down at the book in my hand. It has a coffee stain in the top right corner and as I flick through it, I'm reminded of a bible. I hold it against my chest. "Thank you so much".

Tash rubs my arm, "That was very brave of you, thank you for sharing."

My eyes start to mist again but I smile, "Thank you for being so welcoming." I want to say more but I don't know if this is the time. I get the impression everyone is done sharing for today.

"We are heading off to grab coffee down the road. Do you want to come too?" James is a gentle-looking giant in chef's whites, one clog, and one heavy-duty bandage. You're more than welcome," he says with a smile.

I do feel welcome, but I also want to go and digest some of this book and exhale after what feels like a therapy session.

"Thank you so much," I say. "I've got to get off, though; I'll see you next week."

"Do come back," Janice says. "There are other meetings I run too; they're all listed on the website if you need. This one has stayed outside since covid but there are others inside if it's raining or gets much warmer. You can just come to any of them. I'm also down at the Salvation Army every afternoon this week if you want to drop in. We're here if you need us."

Janice smiles again, making me feel like she's a guidance counsellor at school. I'm a little kid in my school uniform again, and I've just told her all about how the other girls are being awful to me and how I don't get what I've done to upset them. I feel cared for, watched over, and protected.

I feel like serenity could be close.

Cheers! Our reporter Alex Hyndman tries a tas

Drinking on the job

"

God, grant me the
serenity to accept the
things I cannot
change, the courage to
change the things I
can and the wisdom
to know the
difference

CHAPTER 7

Numb

Nine-Thirty AM, 23rd February 2023

Brisbane

510 Days Sober

"Tell me about what you were like as a kid."

I raise my eyebrows, cross and uncross my legs, and then fold my arms across myself. Realising my body language was probably not coming across well, I quickly uncrossed my arms. I started tapping my fingers on the sides of the chairs and scolded myself for not being able to sit still or stop myself from overthinking my non-verbal communication.

"My childhood?" I ask. Dr Robbins, my psychiatrist, sits back in his chair and nods.

"Yes, tell me about your childhood." I wonder if he realises how much of a Freudian cliché that is. Surely, he does.

"I've been trying to remember it, but it's weird; I feel like I'm watching a movie about someone else." I explain. "I remember me when I was younger, but from the outside, not the inside. Does that sound weird?" I ask.

He just nods, so I continue.

"I mean, I always had this feeling, like I was in a movie and I was the main character but I didn't ever understand the other characters' motivations." I'm not sure I'm explaining this properly, I think. "But it's like I felt like me, but I was on a different page to everyone else. I could never understand their actions or their motivations and I'm not sure I understood mine."

I look him in the eye again, but then I feel uncomfortable and start to ramble when he says nothing.

"Still, I know I felt different, like I was special even though I knew I wasn't if that makes sense. I feel like I was acting a part and playing different parts and characters depending on who I was with. It's like I didn't belong, and I was meant to be somewhere else or someone else, but I could never work it out, so I just pretended all the time."

I search the doctor's face for any sign that what I've said makes sense or if it all makes me sound completely mental, but he's giving nothing away.

"What about friends? Did you have close friendships at school?" He asks.

"I don't remember being close to anyone specifically. I never felt like anyone really got me or that I got them. I was thinking about it, and I reckon I copied people I wanted to be friends with when I was trying to fit in."

I look at Dr Robbins; he's giving me nothing, so I continue.

"I didn't ever get the conventions of friendship, and I honestly don't think I do now. I sometimes feel like I'm too much. I give people my whole life story when they ask a simple question, or I jump over them when they talk about something that I can relate to. I annoy myself sometimes in social situations. I reckon I was probably an annoying kid. I remember friends dumping or ghosting me and not understanding why or what I'd done wrong."

"Do you remember what kind of student you were?" He asks.

"Not really, I mean sort of. I looked through my old report cards like you asked, and it seems I was pretty good. I don't remember being constantly in trouble or having a problem in class. I was probably the opposite. Eager to please, putting pressure on myself to get things right. I got good reports but I don't remember feeling smart or capable, more like I either knew it or didn't."

I pick at my fingernails and try to slow down my thoughts so I can answer the question properly.

"I don't remember actively learning until I was much older, then I just tried to cram it all in. I found my old English textbooks. We were allowed to take them into the exams, and I had whole essays written in the tiniest writing in the margins of the books; I'm not sure how I got away with it, but I remember thinking the only way I would get the grades or get through the exams was to find a way to cheat. Which is bizarre, right? If I went to that much trouble writing it all out and trying to hide stuff, why didn't I just spend the time learning the answers? Maybe that was me looking for that bit of danger, do you think? Maybe I was trying to make it harder for myself."

He skips over my questions and heads in a different direction.

"What part do you think your drinking played in all of this, where did that come into play?"

I've told Dr Robbins how I gave up drinking nearly a year and a half ago and how I'm struggling with all the feelings it's brought up. I've told him about how I keep having panic attacks and that no amount of Valium, antidepressants, or HRT seems to be making any difference. I'm having a hard time trying to make sense of all the feelings and I don't think I really know what normal feels like anymore or if I ever did.

"The really heavy drinking started at university. At the time, there was a ladette culture where everyone drank, and a lot of the girls drank like the guys did. I joined the rowing team and hung out at the bar. Then, I trained in the morning and went rowing at 5 am in London in the winter, and then we all drank all the time." I confess.

I looked back at photos of myself, and I was so bloated and swollen, despite the fact I was training and hardly ate. I binged when I drank and sometimes didn't remember to throw up, and passed out, and then I trained again but I couldn't have been doing it properly because I was so big and tired and hungover.

"In my second year, I got sick and was diagnosed with glandular fever and depression, but I don't know. I reckon I had abused my body so badly with all the drinking, smoking, training, starving myself, binging and throwing up, that something had to give."

I feel the weight in me shift after dumping all of that. I do not have a filter and feel uncomfortable like I've accidentally revealed too much.

I try to make eye contact to gauge what he's thinking, but my eyes skip over the top of his head to the painting on the far side of the room. It's all muted blues and greys. I imagine someone thought it would add a calming vibe to the otherwise stark room.

I shift in the mustard yellow armchair and fidget again with my fingernails, picking at my cuticles as I wait for the next question. He looks down at his notepad and scribbles a couple of things before looking up and tapping his pen on the paper a few times.

"Did you stop drinking when you got sick?"

"No, I just kept drinking and going out." I admit.

"I started failing my classes and then got an exchange scholarship to go to university in Melbourne, so I moved there for a year and drank more. I flunked most of my classes, and had a group of friends that I somehow pissed off. I moved back to London and kept drinking and scraped through the end of my degree by the skin of my teeth. I should have done better; I had the potential to be good; I know I did, but I wasted it by getting wasted." I look up and give him a wry smile.

"Were your grades good before that?"

"Yeah, I did well, you know, I was smart—I mean, I *am* smart, but I can't always tap into it." I tell him.

"I can't always make it work, so I did well in the subjects I liked and had to push through some things I wasn't great at, like maths, but I got there. I know I wanted to do well, but I think the whole thing overwhelmed me." I explain.

"I couldn't focus on the important stuff, I couldn't get organised, and I had so few hours where I had to be in lectures that I was bouncing all over the place or bored. I guess it was easier to escape, and yeah, I suppose that was it. I was escaping, shutting down all the doubt, worry, and overwhelm inside my brain, trying to numb it."

"Do you think it worked?"

"Yeah, it worked because I don't have clear memories of that time. It's like I wasn't really there. I know I made some stupid decisions; I was pretty reckless with money and relationships, and I don't remember why or how I ended up where I did.

I try to hide the fact that talking about this version of me is upsetting. It's like I'm talking about someone else, but I feel so strongly connected to her. I'm pretty ashamed about the whole time from university to when I moved back to Australia with the kids. Now that I no longer drink, it's all coming up in dreams and random thoughts. I get flashes of different periods of my life, and I want to try to remember, but at the same time, I don't.

"How does that make you feel?"

"I guess I feel sad for the girl I was." I bite the inside of my mouth to try and stop myself from getting upset.

"It doesn't feel like me," I tell him.

"I feel so sad that she didn't feel like she had anyone and that no one knew how lost she was. No one could help her, and I couldn't help her, and I can't help her now, and I didn't know what was wrong, and it was all so much, and it was such a waste."

Tears are streaming down my face, but I can't stop; it's all just pouring out of me, the hopelessness, the feelings, and the thoughts tumbling out of me like the dam has suddenly been unblocked after years of having a cork jammed in it.

I can see what's happening; I can see it all clearly, and I can't stop crying and talking in a stream of consciousness like I've woken up from a dream or a movie, and I need to get it all out in the fastest way possible.

" It hurts remembering the way I drank more and more to suppress all those feelings, and it makes me sad that I kept doing it even though it didn't help. I couldn't see another way to cope, so I drank more and pushed all the feelings and thoughts down, and I just got further and further away from me, you know? I don't see me there. I don't know where I went, but I don't know who I am, and I'm not sure I've ever known."

I look at Dr Robbins and I want to ask him; *do you know who I am?* But I know that's not how this works. I wish he could tell me. But it's silent in the room I've just filled with all the trapped thoughts I felt stupid for thinking. My words are now floating around this clean white room, bouncing off the walls, searching for answers. I picture them trying to find the first aid kit so they can be wrapped up in a bandage and popped into a hospital bed to be cared for until they're well enough to go back out into the world.

"I've been looking at the results of your DIVA and AQ tests; these are the ones we use for Attention-deficit/Hyperactivity Disorder and Autism Spectrum Disorder diagnosis."

I know these well. My kids have been through this process already, and it's really why I'm here. I need answers, and even though it's making me feel like I'm playing a part again, I think there may be something here.

"I think they show a strong indication for ADHD and ASD, less so for ASD, but it is still present."

He looks at me, and I try to work out what I'm supposed to say; how am I supposed to react?

This is my answer. I think. This is what I've been searching for, what I wanted. There is a reason, an explanation, an excuse for all of my behaviour, my drinking, overspending, and lack of attention. I'm not just useless and dumb, I don't need to be ashamed.

"Right." I sigh.

That's all I can manage to say.

"Ok." He searches my face, "So where we go from here is really up to you."

To the bar? I think to myself and laugh internally, *ha ha, very funny.*

"Which medications are your children on?" He asks.

"They're both on Vyvanse."

"Tolerating it well?"

"Yeah, it seems to be doing what it's supposed to for them."

"Shall we give it a go for you then?"

I leave Dr Robbin's office with scripts for ADHD medication and a new type of SNRI antidepressant and immediately wonder if I just faked all of it.

I sit in the car and start googling.

I open page after page and type all the questions running around my head.

Can you fake an ADHD test?

What happens if you take ADHD medication and don't have ADHD?

Is SNRI better than SSRIs?

Does ADHD medication make you lose weight?

Do SNRIs make you put on weight?

What does ADHD medication do to your sex drive?

I search on and on for answers to questions that run riot in my brain, then make myself stop.

Get a grip, I scold myself in my Mother's voice.

He's a doctor, and I'm sure you're not the first woman with a late diagnosis of ADHD to question whether or not you were playing the part of someone with ADHD.

I decided to give it a go. I mean, I've never been shy about taking drugs before—prescribed or not—so why was I overthinking this?

I head to the pharmacy and fill my script; I'm lucky to have found one stocking the amount I've been given to trial, as there's a worrying shortage.

I read articles about other women like me and scroll through Tik-Tok watching videos about the effects of the medication. Then I search: Are people with ADHD and ASD more likely to be addicts?

I read articles published in The Lancet and The Harvard Gazette, I read one titled, The Truth About ADHD and Addiction in ADDitude magazine and The Hidden Link Between Autism and Addiction in The Atlantic.

The National Library of Medicine has an article published in 2015 that states people with ADHD, "have an increased risk for addiction disorders like alcoholism and substance abuse."

The story in The Atlantic is about a guy who got addicted to heroin because it, "erased his constant anxiety." After going to rehab it says he was diagnosed with autism, which he said was a relief. He said his behaviours, including the addiction, all finally made sense.

The Atlantic article quotes a study in Sweden published on The Springer Link, which suggests people with autism are "more than twice as likely to become addicted to alcohol or other drugs as their peers are." It goes on to say the risk is "even higher for people who also have ADHD."

I sit in the car with the aircon blasting in my face. I'm sweating everywhere, including from my knees. It's thirty degrees outside, but I don't know if I'm sweating from the heat, peri-menopause, or the ADHD meds coursing through my veins. I sit and sweat and imagine the years' worth of shame slowly seeping through my pores.

You can let it go, I tell myself.

It's not your fault.

You're not an addict because you were bored or stupid or made bad choices.

You may have decided to do those things on some level, but you were working against a force so much greater than your choices.

You were so much more likely to get hooked, you didn't know how dangerous it was to start.

It wasn't just because your dad was an alcoholic, it was that but it was all of your undiagnosed mental health conditions too.

You were fighting invisible monsters with demons.

You were never going to win.

The next month is a revelation, I get shit done. I get on top of the laundry and the cooking, and Warren high-fives himself for creating some Stepford wife. I remind him that I am not that by still greeting him with the occasional meltdown as I navigate the meds, the sobriety, the therapy, and the exhaustion brought on by the constant introspection.

I throw myself into researching the conditions and talk to him incessantly about how my ADHD clearly fueled my addiction.

"I'm sorry I didn't realise." He tells me.

"How could you possibly know when I had no idea?" I tell him one night after the kids have finally gone to bed.

We are sitting in the garden next to the fire pit; he's slowly making his way through a glass of red wine, and I'm nursing a cup of tea.

"You weren't to know that I was suffering," I say, trying to reassure him. "I hid it from everyone, including myself. I internalised, then numbed it all until I blacked out and blocked it out repeatedly. It's only now that it's all making some sense."

"I'm just so sorry that I couldn't help you."

He looks so sad. I don't want him to feel like he's failed me. He's such a fixer, and it's the most beautiful thing about him; he always wants to make sure everyone in his life is alright.

"I needed to help myself", I say.

"To get here, I needed to hit rock bottom, make all those mistakes, and then face up to them."

I look into his eyes, and I imagine this amazing man is realising he has taken on way more than he bargained for. He now has a whole house full of people with varying degrees of ADHD and ASD, all trying to find their way in the world, a world that he sees through a completely different lens.

"I wouldn't have found you if I hadn't been on that journey, would I?" I grab his hand. "I know this isn't where we started or where you imagined. I know I'm not drinking red wine with you out here by the fire like you wanted, but I'm here, I'm present, and I love you." I lean over and kiss him.

"Thank you for loving me," I tell him, "that's all I need."

> You were so much more likely to get hooked, you didn't know how dangerous it was to start.

CHAPTER 8

Focus

Eleven Twenty-Three PM, December 14 2023

Greenwich, London

804 days sober

"How did you do it?" I open my messenger app to a note from my friend Tom. We used to work together when I was reading the sports news on TV. Back then, PR firms were constantly inviting us to sporting events. There was always a free bar, way too many drinks, weekends away in Ireland for the golf, Cheltenham and Ascot for the horse racing, and very late nights. I have hazy memories of most of those occasions, tinged with shame about what I might have said or things I might have done.

"I don't think I've got a problem as such," his message continues. "I just don't like the feeling after drinking anymore and I don't know how to stop. What do you suggest?"

I've received a lot of messages like this from people I know, but more from people I don't know but have connected with on social media. I've written a couple of articles about giving up drinking and I started making TikToks and Reels about giving up. At the time, it was more about making myself accountable than giving advice. I don't think it's my place. Everyone is different, right?

There are a lot of sober coaches popping up online, people who claim to have found the secret that they can teach you in just ten easy steps for a subscription fee. *Follow me and join my course to become a better you, find the secret to sobriety,* and *live a life without alcohol.* They all claim to be able to help, and I think in some senses they have their place, but honestly, I'm not a doctor or an addiction expert, and neither are most of them.

I hesitate before I answer. I don't want to preach. I don't know any unique secret. I was addicted to drinking, but I was also addicted to shopping, starving myself, binging, and basically doing anything to make me feel better.

"I stopped by replacing alcohol and changing my habits," I tell him. "I had to cut the alcohol out and start drinking non-alcoholic drinks. Then I had to get some help and support. Have you spoken to anyone else about it?"

I want to be careful not to brush him off, but I also don't want to be too prescriptive. What worked for me might not work for him. I watch the little dots appear as he starts typing back.

"Not really. I talked to my wife Rosie, and she reckons it would be a good idea to cut back, but I've tried that. I was drinking on Fridays and Saturdays, but I ended up drinking way more than I did before and just cramming it all into those two nights and feeling like I'd died on Sunday. Do you think the hangovers get worse the older we get?"

"Totally!" I message back. "The hangovers were so much worse in the past few years than they ever were when we were pulling all-nighters! I reckon it hits us way harder the older we get, and now that we all have kids, we have to get up and deal with them, too, which is an absolute nightmare. Babies and booze do not mix."

I'm trying to keep it fairly light-hearted but I'm a little worried. I know that it takes a lot of guts to reach out and I know he's probably in a bad place if he's asking me for advice. I'm the last person I would imagine people coming to for help, but I guess putting it out there suggests I've got some answers.

"So true," he types back. "Our two little ones are still up a couple of times a night and I want to help, but most nights I've been so blotto that Rosie just gets up and does it herself. Drinking doesn't seem to affect her like it does me. She can stop after a couple; I have no off switch."

"That was always my problem," I quickly type back. "As I'm sure you'll remember, I was always first to the bar and last standing. I always made such a dick of myself. Do you remember our trip to Galway with all those footballers and the big bosses?"

"I do ..." he types and I fire back.

"I shudder when I remember how much I drank and then started singing with the guy playing guitar in the hotel bar. I insisted he play Girls Aloud repeatedly until I got the words right. What song was it again? ..."

"It was Love Machine, and it was hilarious."

Oh god, I think, *he's just being nice.*

It was awful, and I'm still mortified to this day.

Another message pops up.

"We had so much fun. I think we all took it too far sometimes. It feels like it's time to grow up now."

"Asking for help and acknowledging that I was done with drinking was the biggest step for me. Knowing that I wanted to stop and finding different ways of helping make it stick took a lot of effort, but it was worth it."

"What did you do though?"

He wants a list, a prescriptive list of steps, and I get it, but I don't have a formula.

I'm worried about telling him to do one thing or another when I have no real insight into what his life or drinking looks like these days. I start chewing on my fingernail and think, if I could break it down into steps, what would I say?

"OK, these are just some suggestions." I write

"You have to find what works for you and get to a doctor to talk through whether you need some other support. In the meantime, find a non-alcoholic drink you like and have that at home. Get rid of all the stuff you'd normally reach for when you feel the urge to have a drink and have as many of them as you want. Then get some sugar. I ate so many sweets to start with, and it really helped me. Think about what triggers you to have a drink. When do you usually start drinking on a regular day?"

"Lunchtime," he types, followed by an emoji of a monkey with his hands over his eyes.

"No judgement here; my favourite saying was *It's five o'clock somewhere* when it was normally breakfast time. So, when it gets to lunchtime, try to avoid the craving for a drink by drinking something else. If you're out to lunch, find out what's on their drinks list before you go. I sometimes ring a restaurant before going there to ensure they have something. I found it hard to drink fizzy water at the start, but tonic water was a good substitute for me if that was the only option."

"OK, sounds like a plan. What else?"

"You got any hobbies? Still playing golf or tennis?"

"Yeah, still try to get in a round of golf."

"Do it more!" I enthuse. "Just make yourself too busy to think about drinking and then start counting the days so you can congratulate yourself."

"What if I fuck up though? I would feel so crap if I started this and couldn't stick to it."

"Please don't be so hard on yourself. If you have a drink, go back to day one. Take it one day at a time. Just message me whenever you need me. I'm always here, and I while haven't got all of the answers, I do get it, I've been there, and I know it's worth it. You've got this."

I send him a strong-arm emoji, shut off my phone, and close my eyes, our conversation playing repeatedly in my head. I'm worried about giving out advice. I want to be helpful, but I don't have all the answers, I'm still working it out for myself.

I can't sleep, so I grab my phone and roll over onto my side. I flick the bedside light on and breathe in the scent of lavender from the little bowl next to the lamp.

I send Warren a good morning message, telling him I love him and am counting the days until we see each other. He's working in Brisbane and will meet the kids and me in New York on Boxing Day. We have a big trip planned after we visit London. We're hoping it will distract the kids from their initial sadness whenever they leave London and head back to the other side of the world.

I'm staying at my friend Michelle's house in London while she's visiting her family in Australia. Her dog Monty is curled up at my feet. I've left the curtains open and can see over the tops of the terraced houses and to the Dome and the lights on the skyscrapers of Canary Wharf.

Whenever I'm here, the sights, smells, and sounds transport me back to when I was married to Geoff, when the children were babies, and I would push them along the dirty streets of West Greenwich in the double buggy. I used to feel overwhelmed by sadness and regret, but I realise it's slowly fading.

I'm not quite strong enough to walk past the house we renovated or point it out to the children and tell them it's where they first lived when they were babies. I sometimes picture myself knocking on the door, but I know my heart can't handle that yet. Seeing someone else living the future we had tried to build for ourselves would be too traumatic. But being here and seeing the skyline from a different bedroom is somehow comforting.

This will always be a home for me and the kids; it houses the memories of their dad, his life, and his spirit will always live here. He never managed to visit us in Brisbane, which is why I think it's easier for the kids to get by day to day without being jolted by memories of him. There are photos of him all over their bedrooms, but it's not a place he has ever inhabited. Here, there are memories of him on every corner, but with each year that passes, I'm beginning to feel a fondness for those memories rather than feeling like I've been punched in the stomach.

The only thing that is more difficult to reconcile is how much he is missing, how much Alfie and Olivia have grown up, and how much he would have loved to see that. Seeing life go on without him is painful, but overall, the children are much more settled this time. They're staying with their nana, Geoff's mum and spending time with their half-sister Emily and their step-mum Nat; I've also been welcomed into family events. I think we are all in a much better place.

I blink away tears at the thought of the children becoming little adults and my privilege in seeing them become real people. Geoff would be so proud of them.

I open Instagram and look back through the messages I've received over the past two years. I've been posting a lot about being sober, losing

Geoff, feeling all the feelings and facing up to addiction and the reasons behind it. I have been doing a lot of work with my counsellor and talking through all the reasons I drank and all the ways life is better now that I don't drink. I still don't feel qualified to dish out advice, but I also know how hard it is to find the right help.

When I first wanted to give up, I spent hours trying to find out where rehab centres were, how much they cost, and which ones were government-funded. The path to sobriety is not well signposted, and so many unknowns exist. I had a long list of worries about admitting I had a problem or going to rehab. I stressed myself out thinking irrational things like *Will they take my kids away if I tell them how much I drink? Will they send me away? Will they lock me up?*

I don't know who *they* are in this scenario, but I distinctly remember being terrified of all of the possibilities despite my relatively privileged position. I could afford to spend the money if I needed to. My husband, mum or sister would have helped with the kids, but the worst-case scenarios still petrified me.

I also questioned whether my drinking problem was bad enough to need rehab. There wasn't a scale, as far as I could tell, that allowed me to work out how much of a risk I was taking by going cold turkey and giving sobriety a go on my own.

I feel like I was very lucky to have managed to stay alcohol-free without the medical help that I honestly think I needed but was too scared to access. The place I found myself, though, was a kind of no-man's land; I had to choose my own adventure when it came to getting sober. I decided to go it alone because I was too scared to reach out properly. I wish I had put my hand up high and said *Please help me..*

I scroll through my messages. So many are from women reaching out after reading about my rock bottom and my decision to get sober. I still feel embarrassed about putting so much of my life out in public, but reading the message reminds me why I did it and why I need to keep doing it. Even though I only have a small platform, I know that using my words is what I do best; it makes me want to write more and more.

They say things like Congratulations, I'm sober too."

"My husband died, and I drank too,"

"You've given me hope."

"Thank you so much for sharing."

"So much of your story resonated with me."

"Your story was my story."

"You have done an incredibly selfless service by telling your story."

"You will help guide other women out of their shame and help their kids heal."

I've replied to them and even spoken to some on the phone. I try not to give out too much advice as I don't think that's why people want to connect. I think they just want to feel like they're not alone, like it's not just them who has a problem with alcohol I think they are searching for other people who understand, like I was. I think they want to connect and talk about how hard it is despite knowing they are doing the best thing they can for themselves, for their kids, for their partners, for their jobs, and for their whole lives.

I scroll through my Instagram, which is now almost exclusively sober people, non-alcoholic drinks companies, and charities, with the odd fashion and beauty brand thrown in for a bit of balance. My feed is populated by white squares with black writing conveying affirmations like *Sobriety is cool*. There are motivational quotes about sharing stories and being there for others who want to get sober too.

My feed says things like :

Tell people you got sober. You might be the only sign of hope they have.

Share your sobriety with others.

You can't be what you can't see.

Shame dies when you shine a light on it.

There is a whole world of sober people out there who aren't anything like the image I had of them before. I never imagined they were like me. I thought they were clean living wellness gurus who'd once slept on a park bench but had now found God, seen the light and embraced religion to break free from addiction. That's a cliché, a stereotype that does exist, but it's not the whole story or the only one.

I see shiny influencer faces, famous faces, and smart people who have held down careers while drinking but are now soaring to greater heights since they've quit drinking.

Some people credit quitting drinking as the reason they are here at all, some just say they feel better without booze.

I certainly do, but laying in this gorgeous bed in London, all cosy and warm and wrapped in the unbelievable hospitality of my beautiful friend and snuggling with her beloved dog. I feel a warm glow of gratitude, I'm so grateful for where I am right now. I take a minute to reflect on how much of a difference it has made to me having a supportive partner and family. I've found the right combination of supportive friends, a counsellor, a psychiatrist, a diagnosis, and answers. I can see a way forward and a future that looks very different to the train wreck my life could have been. But what if just one piece of that puzzle were missing? I wonder. What then?

I've had a message from another Mum who I knew from my kid's primary school in Melbourne. Lucy's been struggling and has messaged me a couple of times before asking general questions, but this time it's slightly more concerning.

"Hi Lex, just wondering when you're back and if you'd mind if I tagged along to an AA meeting with you?"

I haven't been to an AA meeting in a while. I found it helpful to see I wasn't alone and that there was a supportive group there but, in the end, I felt like I didn't need to keep going.

"Hey lovely, great to hear from you. Yes, of course I will. I'm not back until the end of January. Shall we get together when the kids are back at school?"

I hit send and then start to worry. If she's in a bad enough place to be reaching out, then maybe she needs help sooner rather than later. I quickly type a follow-up message.

"You ok? Want to chat?"

"I'm ok," she replies. "Just been drinking way too much over the holidays, and I can't seem to stop. I think it's time to get some help."

"I understand, but do you need help right now? I'm worried about you."

She doesn't respond. I'm concerned because I'm guessing she's finding things more challenging than she's likely to let on. The fact that she's messaging me early in the morning Australian time suggests she's had a big night and is probably in a bad place mentally.

I know how dark I felt in those moments, how hopeless and desperate a hangover after weeks of drinking too much could be. The anxiety and self-loathing I felt on those mornings after a long weekend of overindulging was often verging on dangerous. I want to make sure she gets help, but I don't want to cross a line and push her away or make her feel worse than she already does.

I wait a few more minutes and then decide to send her the link to ADIS, it's the 24/7 Alcohol and Drug support line I hope sending her the number is the best way to give her a little push in the right direction. I'm worried that she needs help before I can get back to her and help her go to a meeting.

I have visions of her spiralling and going on one last bender. As it's the holidays, it's more likely her kids could see her wasted like mine did. I don't wish that shame on anyone. I see that she has read my message but not replied so I send a message with love heart emojis to her, put my phone on silent, snuggle up to Monty and finally fall asleep.

The next morning, I wake up to a message from Lucy. "I called them; the counsellor was lovely. I've got a referral to do outpatient detox and then rehab."

I quickly type back, hoping she's still awake. I've made the most of being on my own and have slept in, it's late at night back in Australia.

"Lucy, that's brilliant news. You have done the right thing by reaching out for help. You are so brave, and you have got this. I am always here for you."

Text messages don't convey how much my heart is swelling with pride for her and with the feeling that I have helped someone. I'm overcome with how much has changed in my life. I used to only be able to see myself, but now I can see outside myself and finally have the mental strength to think about people who might need help and not just struggle to keep my head above water.

66

Tell people you got sober. You might be the only sign of hope they have.

CHAPTER 9

Goodbye

Eight Twenty-Five AM, 28th December 2022

Borough, London, England

"You ruined everything," he says, looking at me with furious intensity. "Why did you take us away? Why did you take me from my whole family and ruin my whole life? Why?"

I have no idea what to say to this little boy, my darling son, whom I want to be so proud of for voicing his honest thoughts and feelings, but I'm so taken aback that I'm struggling to find the words. We've been in London for a few weeks, and it's the first time we've been back here since his dad died. I knew it would be challenging, but I hadn't prepared myself for the anger Alfie is feeling or for it to be directed at me.

"I'm sorry, baby. I'm so sorry." I look at him and fight the urge to defend myself, to tell him that I am the adult and did what I had to do, what I thought was right. My apology isn't cutting it, though. He has burning questions, and he is demanding answers.

"My whole family is here. Why did you take me away?" It breaks my heart to see Alfie like this. He's infuriated with me, and he has every right to be. I try to hold back the tears as he starts angrily wiping his own away with the inside of his t-shirt. I can see so much of his father in his beautiful face; he is like a mini-Geoff. I reach out to brush his mop of dark brown hair away from his deep chocolate eyes, which are reddening from all of the furious wiping. He pushes my hand away.

Warren and Olivia have gone out to pick up some breakfast and it's just us in the Airbnb we've rented near Borough Market. It's the kind of place I was desperate to live in before. Geoff and I talked about it a lot, but like many things we both wanted, it never happened.

"Your dad and I tried to work it out. You were so little, darling, I didn't know what the right thing to do was." I try to explain, but it all sounds hollow like I'm trying to hide something when I'm not. I tell him I'm sorry and can't change the past, but he wants a different answer. He wants me to fix something I can't.

"But why couldn't you just stay here so I could see him, why did you do it?"

I thought it was the right thing to do. I'm so sorry, baby." I wish I could explain it to him in a way he could understand or even partially accept". I want to tell him I needed to move on with my life. I wish I could tell him that I know my decisions cost him the life he is imagining, but all I can tell him is that I'm sorry.

His stare is piercing, and his fury isn't subsiding at all. If anything, he's getting angrier and as much as I want to run away I know I need to sit here and take it.

"But you took us away, you took me away from my dad, and now he's gone. How could you?"

"Alfie, I didn't know Daddy was going to get sick and die. I thought he would get better. I didn't know we'd be in the middle of a pandemic and it would be so hard to travel. I moved back home to Australia because I wanted to be close to my family and for you two to grow up like I did, going to the beach and playing outside. I wanted you to grow up travelling and being able to see the world, not stuck in the smog and pollution in London, never seeing the ocean."

I rattle off my list of reasons, the things I've explained to him before, the things I thought were important when I packed up our lives and moved us to the other side of the world. I can hear his dad's voice berating me for choosing these things over him. *Why did I think these things were more important than being close to their dad?* I had just wanted to escape, but how do I explain that to Alfie? Geoff wasn't an awful man I had to run from. He wasn't the husband or partner I needed, but he wasn't an evil man. Telling my son that it just didn't work out between us isn't enough for him. I want him to understand but know I'm fighting a losing battle. He will only ever see it from his perspective, and that's ok, I tell myself. It's ok for him to be angry. It's ok.

"I just wanted my dad. I don't care about traveling, Australia isn't my home, and I don't care about the stupid beach. I just wanted to be with him, and now I can't be ever again, and it's all your fault."

I can't help it; my face and my resolve crumble. I can't keep up the façade and burst into tears. "I'm sorry, baby, I'm so sorry."

Alfie and I have had a version of this conversation many times before. He's asked me why, normally from the back of the car when it's just us. I've tried to explain a million different ways, but as much as I know he will never understand, he will probably never forgive me. I tell him over and over again that he is allowed to be angry and it's normal to be sad and upset about things that have happened to him, especially losing his dad. He is going to grieve and rage against the unfairness of it all. I tell him that's normal and that it's not fair, none of it is, but of course, it doesn't help. I know that he is struggling and will focus most of that anger on me, but it doesn't stop me feeling terrible. It hurts so much to see my boy in so much pain and feel responsible for it.

Before Geoff died, I drank to deal with my pain, guilt and shame. I used it to push down the voices in my head. Drinking dulled the pain inflicted by Alfie's fury and resentment and replaced it with numbness, blankness and eventual blackout. I didn't want to face the pain I'd caused him then, and I don't want to face it today, but now there's no escape. I swallow down my feelings and try to hug him. He pushes me away. I shift slightly away from him on the couch and stare at the Christmas tree the owners have left for us in the flat. It reminds me of our first Christmases when they were babies, and how I had thought our life, our family, and their childhood would all be so very different.

This trip back tp London is hard but one of the things that is making it even harder for the kids is that we are going to be burying Geoff's ashes at the cemetery. It's called internment, and it will be kind of like his funeral. I can't imagine it and don't know how to prepare them or myself to see an urn being put into the ground. I wonder if it's better or worse than seeing a coffin. Seeing an urn full of ashes makes me imagine a body being burned and the awful imagery that goes with that. I always thought I wanted to be cremated, but now I hate that idea.

The kids have been given little urns, and it makes me feel sick; I can't help picturing Geoff inside. I don't like the idea of them having an urn with his ashes in their bedroom at home. I can't get my head around it, but I don't say any of this to them. The most precious thing they have been given are pendants with Geoff's fingerprint. I think that's a beautiful way to keep him close, but I can also picture them taking prints from his dead body, and that makes me feel creeped out, too. I just can't believe he's dead and that their connection to their dad is now reduced to small keepsakes. They only have broken memories of him when he was properly alive, before he got sick, before they saw him unable to walk or heard him throwing up at night after chemo. I want them to remember him like he was before cancer,. I want them to be able to say goodbye but I can't believe he's gone then I know they will be struggling. I can still hear his voice and the way he said their names. I wish I could save those memories instead of taking home a pile of ashes.

"Why can't we just stay?" Alfie still has questions. His questions are what a much younger child might blurt out. It's like his emotional age is stunted by everything he's been through.

"Baby, Daddy isn't here anymore. We have a life in Australia."

"I want to stay here."

"I'm sorry, we can't."

He storms off to the bedroom and slams the door behind him. I can hear him throwing things around the room, but I don't stop him. I just sit and look at the tree and let the silent tears stream down my face. I crave the sweet escape of a drink and imagine opening one of the bottles calling me from the wine fridge. I grab the non-alcoholic spirits I brought at Whole Foods, the one that is supposed to induce calm, and pour myself a glass and fill it with ice.

I spend the entire three weeks either crying or struggling to hold back tears. I know this has a lot to do with removing alcohol. I no longer have my coping mechanism and I'm having to feel all the feelings and sit with them no matter how uncomfortable it is. I know this is healthy. I've read about how important it is for me to work through this period of grief and deal with all the trauma, but God, it's so difficult.

I'm still processing my feelings about how we ended our marriage and how I moved away with the kids, and I don't know how to begin processing his death. I keep expecting him to be here, in all these familiar places. I see his ghost in the bars and restaurants where we spent our first dates, in the streets around our first home, at his mum's house. All the family's homes are full of pictures of him looking out at me from every wall. He's smiling and dancing, there are pictures of him at our wedding and with the kids when they were little, and there are photos of him at work, meeting the Queen and the Prime Minister. They are like shrines to him. There are no pictures of us together, no photos of me anywhere. It's understandable, but it still makes me feel like the part I played in his life has been erased.

Antidepressants and Valium are propping me up, but nothing could have prepared me for the overwhelming grief I'm hit with when I turn up at the cemetery on a cold, rainy January day. I've driven myself there in a hire car after insisting that Warren didn't need to come. Geoff's sister Laura, who hasn't spoken to me for years, is there with her husband. Their two boys are there too. They're my nephews, but they're strangers to me now, and they only know me as Alfie and Olivia's mum; I'm not Aunty Lex anymore. Our boys were all born so close together and I had imagined they'd grow up playing football and hanging out constantly. Alfie would have loved that.

The children arrive with their half-sister Emily, Geoff's mum and his widow Nat in a funeral car. My chest tightens as I walk across the muddy grass to reach them. I struggle with my umbrella in the wind and my inappropriate high-heeled boots in the mud. Olivia searches my face as I get closer, clearly trying to gauge my emotional state. I hold out my hand and bring her into a half hug. Alfie's expression is blank as he looks at me. He walks past and stands by his dad's grave with his cousins.

Geoff's mum Pauline has brought flowers in the shape of a football, in Crystal Palace's red, white and blue colours. She places them on the spot where his ashes are going to be buried. I lean over and rub her arm as I see her start crying. She has taken his death so hard; they were incredibly close, and seeing him suffer and then losing him in such an awful way has completely devastated her.

At his gravesite, there's a hole in the ground that seems inadequately small. There's also a wooden cross with a gold plaque on it. It reads: *Geoff*

Hill, 1969-2021, A dearly loved Father, Son, Brother and Husband—a wonderful man who is missed every day.

I stare at it and can't match the man that I married twelve years ago to this place. None of this feels real, I'm not ready to say goodbye. I had never pictured him in a grave, a place where the kids would come and visit him, a final resting place.

I'm numb with cold and sadness, I'm trying to stop shivering as I hold an umbrella over Pauline's head. Silent tears stream relentlessly down my face and Olivia keeps glancing at me and looking concerned. I try to give her a half smile and urge her with a nod not to worry about me. It's not about me, I feel like it's not even my place to cry. I don't deserve to be mourning, do I?

I wonder what his family really think, whether they think I have a right to be sad. I know I made Geoff sad—we made each other sad—but we also shared so much happiness. I try to picture the happy times, making a mental note to talk more about them with the children when we are all together again. They're going to be staying with Geoff's mum for the remainder of our trip and I'm so worried about them being upset and not having me to comfort them. I'm also grateful for the break, grateful that his family are sharing the burden and that maybe some of Alfie's anger will dissipate over time.

I look around, and no one is meeting my eye, all their heads are bowed, and everyone is looking sadly at the mound of earth. I can feel the weight of their grief. I feel so much responsibility for it. I know I didn't make him sick, but I know that nothing I did after we split up made any part of his life easier. The only comfort I take is that he married Natalie. That was who he was meant to be with. She has been so strong through his illness, and she's always been there for the kids. She has done everything to support them and make them feel loved and included.

I look at her and marvel as she reads a poem with a steady voice. I couldn't have been that strong. I wouldn't have survived the things she has been through. She signals to the vicar who is leading this little service, and he presses play on the stereo, which I hadn't noticed next to the cross. U2's song *One* blasts out, breaking into the cold air. I look at the children and try to calm my breathing, sucking in air and puffing my cheeks so I don't start wailing. Bono's voice fills the silence and I realise I've never listened to the song's words properly before.

"Is it getting better?

Or do you feel the same?

Will it make it easier on you now?

You got someone to blame."

"Did I disappoint you?

Or leave a bad taste in your mouth?

You act like you never had love and you want me to go without.

Well, it's too late, tonight, to drag the past out into the light.

Have you come here for forgiveness?

Have you come to raise the dead?"

I barely hold it together as the small congregation walks away from the site. Everyone hugs before they pile back into the car. I awkwardly give everyone a hug and a kiss, saying repeatedly, "I'm so sorry."

I tell them all, the children, his sister and her husband, his daughter Emily, his mum, "I'm sorry," but I know it will never be enough. They are all leaving in the car to have lunch together somewhere. I'm left standing in the cold, shell-shocked and lost.

I get in the car and drive with the music turned up loud to drown out the thoughts in my head. I realise I can barely see the road because I'm crying so hard, so I pull over and call Karen. I'm close to her place and pray she answers. I'm sobbing uncontrollably when she picks up.

"Lex? I can't understand what you're saying. What's happened?"

"Sorry," I say again. "I'm round the corner," I snivel. "Can you come and meet me?"

"Yes, darling, of course. Meet me at Gail's in Blackheath, I'll be there in 10."

I feel better and worse all at once. Calling up a friend like that and having them drop everything to meet me is something I used to take for granted. When I lived here, it was normal. Now I live so far away that I don't have that. I haven't got those sorts of friends in Brisbane yet, and I wonder if I ever will.

I arrive before her and order from behind my dark sunglasses, which are totally out of place on this dreary day. I find a seat as far away from everyone else as possible, and when Karen walks in, I burst into tears again.

"You need pastry," she declares and briefly hugs me before heading back to the counter. She returns with the most delicious-looking pain au raisin, and I realise it's been hours since I've eaten anything. I start ripping it apart and the whole story tumbles out of me in between mouthfuls of flaky, buttery pastry. She was right; I did need this; it's filling a hole inside me.

"Don't blame yourself for any of this; you didn't make him sick, you didn't ruin anything, you did what was best for you, and you deserve to be happy," she says, protesting my affirmations that my existence has somehow caused everyone's misery. "Those children deserve to have a happy Mum, and I know it is all shit right now, but you will get through this, and you will be strong for them, and they will be fine. You will be fine."

"Thank you. I'm sorry. Again, I keep saying sorry. I just can't seem to keep my feelings in check. They're just all up here and coming out of here." I point to the top of my head and my still streaming eyeballs. "I can't stop feeling all the feelings."

"That's normal and that's way better than you were before. I was really worried about you when you were last here. You were drinking way too much, you were a mess, and now you're still a mess, but you're a mess for a good reason. You're processing the trauma, but you will get through this and drinking was never going to help you do that."

Karen has always been one of my best, no-nonsense friends. She says it how she sees it, but I'm slightly shocked to hear her say she was worried about me. I'm glad she's telling me, but I thought I'd done an excellent job of pretending to be ok. I don't want to go back to being like that: drunk and unpredictable. I know that getting sober is worth it, and knowing that I was worrying my friends makes me even more determined never to go back.

I meet Cristina and Amy for dinner that night, and despite my best efforts and promises to myself not to do it, I burst into tears when I walk in and see their faces. I start apologising again as I fumble with my coat and bag, trying to hide my face from the people at other tables turning around to assess my dramatic entrance. I'm sniffling and rubbing at the ever-present mascara smudge that now lives beneath my lower lashes.

"I'm sorry, God, I'm going to stop, I promise. I honestly don't know why I can't stop crying. Sorry," I say.

"Don't be stupid, Lex," Amy grabs my hand and helps me slide next to her in the booth, "Don't be so stupid, it's fine. We've seen you in a worse state than this before." She nudges me and raises an eyebrow, waiting for me to smile. They know me too well. I have turned up to countless dinners with them after all day drinking, reeking of alcohol, slurring my words, constantly late. At least now I'm not making a drunken scene, just a tearful one.

They've ordered mezze and a bottle of non-alcoholic wine, and they fill my glass and push food towards me as I fill them in on the whole day. I drain my glass as I tell them how awful it was seeing the kids and feeling separate from them and responsible for their pain, how I was left standing on my own, how I don't want to cry on Warren's shoulder anymore and how I need to get it together. Even though I know there's no alcohol in the drink, the action of holding a wine glass and drinking through my story is making me feel so much better. I'm grateful that bars and restaurants in London have bought into the whole non-alcoholic movement just in time for me to ditch drinking.

"You've been through a lot, and you're allowed to be upset. It would frankly be weird if you weren't. This is a huge trip, and you've got a lot to deal with." Cristina and Amy have seen me through everything. They knew me when the kids were little, even before Alfie was born, and I can always depend on them, even when I'm spiralling.

"I just feel like a real drink would help right now." I pause for effect and see their faces drop. "I'm joking, guys."

"Ha ha," says Amy, "You are doing so well; it would all be worse if you were drinking. You'd just be putting off the inevitable. You have to feel this to get through it. It will be worth it."

"But am I boring now I don't drink?" I know it's pathetic that I'm asking, especially when bigger issues are at play. But these are my girls, the girls I've always had a drink with, the girls I've shared some of the most ridiculously fun nights with, the girls I've been away on long, boozy, hilarious weekends with. I know it's dumb, but I need reassurance from people who knew the old me.

"You are so much better without booze. Honestly, you are more present and easier to be around."

I look at Cristina, "Really?"

"Yes," she agrees. You are so much better without it. Starting drinking again wouldn't help you right now. It would make everything worse. We are so proud of you; you're doing so well."

My heart swells. "I'm so sorry you guys had to deal with drunk me; I'm so lucky to have you."

"You don't have to apologise."

"But I do, I feel like I should apologise to everyone. I know I'm not doing the whole AA thing, but that part of it, the part where you're supposed to make amends, I feel like I need to do that. I want to make amends for all the shit I put you two through. I want to make up for the times I let alcohol take centre stage. Like that time in Milan when I was so drunk, I made us get dressed up to go to a club, then was so messed up that you had to put me to bed. Or the time during COVID, when I dragged you both around the freezing cold streets to find pubs serving takeaway so I could drink pints of mulled wine until we could barely stand up. I can't believe all the times I ordered stupidly expensive bottles of wine at lunch, and you always split the bill with me even when I drank most of it. I feel awful, and I want to make up for it; I don't want to be that person. I want to be a proper friend. I love you guys so much." I'm crying again. "I'm sorry," I blub, rooting around in my bag for tissues and another Valium.

"Stop, it's all ok. We were there with you and made our own decisions about drinking with you. It was fun at the time, but it is still fun without it. Not today, obviously, today you are no fun at all." Amy smiles at me. I appreciate her attempts to drag me out of my self-pity, and I know what I need to do.

"Will you guys come with me to The Southwark Tavern?"

"The pub? Why?" Cristina asks.

"It's where Geoff and I had most of our first dates. I think it's time to say goodbye properly."

I realise that I couldn't say goodbye properly at the cemetery. It didn't feel right, but I reckon this is what he would have wanted. It'll be like a wake. I need to say goodbye to him in a place where we have good memories, and I need to say goodbye to that drinking part of my life too.

"

Is it getting better, or
do you feel the same?
Will it make it easier
on you now you've got
someone to blame?
Did I disappoint you,
or leave a bad taste in
your mouth?

CHAPTER 10

Amends

Eleven AM, May 23rd 2021

Brisbane, Australia

T he kids have a lot of questions this morning. Questions I don't know how to answer. Questions like, "Mummy, do you remember walking up the hill without your shoes on? Do you remember when you fell? Does your bottom still hurt? Your eyes looked so funny last night. You were on my bed and you were bopping Oscar on the nose and giggling, do you remember? Mummy, we didn't go to bed until 1 a.m. Why did you make us stay out so late?"

I can't answer any of these questions, I can't work out how to explain the previous night's complete lapse in judgment. I don't have any excuses; I don't remember much of it. I'm struggling to focus, my head is pounding, and I feel awful about what they've seen, what I said and did. I can barely move, so I order McDonald's delivery for breakfast in a vain attempt to divert their attention from my deathly appearance and try and cure my hideous hangover.

Warren is away on a business trip in Sydney, and I'm supposed to be taking Olivia to a bowling alley birthday party for one of her soccer mates. "How the hell am I going to get through today," I wonder as I drag myself into the shower and turn it on full blast to try and cover up the sound of my vomiting.

It had started as a normal enough night, I remember there were cocktails, margaritas and espresso martinis. My white jacket had coffee stains all down the front, so there were definitely espresso martinis. "Oh god," I groan as the coffee I've just inhaled decides to reappear.

I hug the toilet bowl until I'm sure there's no more coffee and then slide onto the cold tiles with my phone. I rest my cheek on the floor, willing the throbbing in my temples to subside. I squint at the phone light and scroll through my photos and text messages, searching for clues. I look at the messages to Warren and see the last few, which I have no recollection of sending. I gasp when I realised that Olivia sent them at two in the morning.

"Warren, it's Olivia; I'm worried about Mummy," the last one reads, "she is acting so weird, and I'm scared."

Fuck, fuck, fuck, what have I done?

I call Warren and bite hard on my lip as I wait for him to answer.

"Hey babe, you ok?" He sounds chirpy enough, not angry or worried, so that's good.

"Yeah, I'm ok, kind of. I had a big one last night with the rugby mums, and I feel awful. The kids ended up staying with me at Josie's until late. I just saw some texts that Liv sent you."

"Right," he says and goes quiet. I can tell he's put me on speaker to look at the messages. "Is everything ok? Is she alright now? What was she worried about?"

"I was drunk; I'm sorry, I think I scared them being so wasted. I don't know how I got so out of it." That's a lie, I know how. I had too many drinks.

"Don't worry, they'll be ok, as long as you're alright."

"I'm fine. I mean, I'm dying, obviously, but it's my own doing, so I've got to suck it up and get through today."

"You going to be ok to drive?" Shit, I hadn't thought about that. "No, probably not; I'll have to get an Uber there. Bugger."

"OK, be safe, got to go." He hangs up, and I prise myself off the floor and mentally prepare to walk upstairs and get dressed.

The Uber ride is an exercise in breathing control or, rather, vomit control. I manage to keep it down until we get to the bowling alley, then I make my excuses and thrust the kids towards the birthday girl and race towards the toilets. I hurl and can't do anything to cover the sound as I see tiny pairs of feet in the stalls on either side of me.

Dear God, I'm setting the best example for everyone's kids today.

I make small talk with some of the mums and then find a dark corner where I slowly sip a full-fat Coke and try to eat a couple of Alfie's chips. Liv seems oblivious and is having fun with her friends, who are all struggling to pick up the massive bowling balls and giggling.

That night, I feel like I might have gotten away it without them asking me any more questions, but Liv brings it up again. She's still concerned and wants to talk about the events of last night. It's the last thing I want to do, and I want just to brush it off and tell her not to worry, but I know she will stress, and then she'll probably tell someone else. What do they do to mums who drunkenly drag their kids through the streets in the early hours of the morning when they can barely stand up? Would her teacher tell social services if she mentioned it in class? I can't risk it. My mind is going to some very dark places, places where I lose my kids. I have to put an end to her worrying about me and try and stop her talking about what happened.

Olivia keeps mentioning it. She brings it up every day for the first couple of weeks. She asks if my shoulder is okay and if I am feeling alright. She asks if I am going to drink again if I am going to get drunk tonight or tomorrow, and if I have managed to get the coffee stains out of my coat.

"Do you remember?" she keeps asking, expecting me to somehow have found my memory and have now pieced together the events of that night. She tells Warren about what happened and asks him why he didn't answer her phone calls when she was scared. "It was the middle of the night, I'm sorry darling," he tells her sweetly, "I was fast asleep."

I tell her that if she's ever really worried about someone in the future she needs to call triple zero, but I tell her that I won't get drunk again, so she won't have to worry about me getting into that state. Secretly, I wonder if that is a promise I can keep. I don't have an off switch and can never stick to one or two drinks. How am I going to make a promise like that unless I stop drinking completely? But maybe I can have just one now and then; I try and reason with myself and promise I'll get a handle on my drinking. I know I won't be able to moderate. I know myself, and even though I don't want to face it, I know that I have to stop drinking for good this time.

A few weeks after Geoff dies, I'm ready to face up to my mistakes, and I sit the kids down to talk about my drinking again. They've been struggling so much with coming to terms with his death and I've been drinking more and more again, seeking oblivion when my kids desperately need me in the present.

Warren and I talk to them over dinner about the science behind being drunk. We talk about how alcohol affects people differently, how getting drunk can depend on things like how much you've eaten, if you're used to alcohol, what you're drinking and how much. We explain to them that being drunk can creep up on you because your body is still metabolising the drinks long after you've had them.

"If you've had, say, three glasses of wine, you might feel perfectly fine in that moment, but your body hasn't had time to process all of the alcohol, especially if you've been drinking quickly and you haven't eaten much. You might feel really happy and giddy and think that another drink is a great idea, but by the time the fourth drink is being metabolised, you could be completely drunk. That's where the bad decisions live; you can do or say things you wouldn't normally do or say and even blackout. That's where people can find yourself in a scary situation, no matter how old you are or who you're with. I don't want to scare you guys, but I want to tell you that I know how bad my decisions about drinking have been lately and that's because I haven't been thinking about the consequences. It's not fair on you and I need to change things."

"I know the world doesn't make much sense to you guys right now," Warren says. "The things that have happened to you, like losing your dad, are unfair. We want to make sure you feel as safe and cared for as possible."

"I'm so sorry about all the times I've made you uncomfortable," I tell them. "I'm sorry we took you to places where people have been drinking and made you feel unsafe. I'm sorry for all the times I've been drunk around you and made you feel like you weren't important. I should never drink like that, and I'm sorry. I'm going to do my best to make some changes. I promise."

The promise scares me. I don't want to lie to them. I want nothing more than to make sure it never happens again, but I know how ingrained drinking is in my life. I want to stop. I need to stop. I have to stop for them, but I must also stop for myself. I can't sit here explaining how much damage alcohol can do, telling them I know how much damage it has already done to our family and keep doing it. I want my children to feel safe. I don't want them to worry about losing me, too; I don't want them to have to worry about me at all. I can't make the pain of losing their dad go away; I can't make it better, but surely, I can do my darndest not to do things that will make them feel worse.

So I stop.

I stop drinking cold turkey.

I note the date on a sober app and count the hours and days that I haven't had a drink. I'm proud of myself, and I see the changes. I won't pretend that it's not hard, it is so hard, and I struggle, but I don't break my promise to myself or them. I don't drink anymore.

After I've been sober for a few months, I decide to talk to the kids about it some more. I want to solidify it for them. I want to hear how they feel about the night I got drunk and everything that's happened since. I want to help them transition, work through it all, and make amends for the mistakes and damage I've caused. I've been reading about ways to help kids deal with grief and trauma and hope that employing some of these strategies will help them heal.

I know that seeing me drunk once probably isn't the most traumatic thing they have gone through, but it's left a mark. Everything I've read says I should give them space to talk uninterrupted and let them lead the conversation about what has happened and what they experienced. I'm scared, but I know that by letting them talk, creating a safe space for them to express themselves and be heard is so important, no matter how much it hurts me. I hope it will help heal me, too.

We drive to the beach, and after we've walked the dogs and had some time just being together, I sit them in the back of the car. Before we head home, I say I want to chat about how they're feeling. I ask them if I can film myself talking to them about me giving up drinking just in case it's helpful for anyone else, and they agree. I keep them out of shot and start my phone recording, focused on me. I start by asking Olivia what she remembers about the last time I was drunk. She tells me what she remembers and how it made her feel, and I listen.

"You were walking up the hill in your heels and stuff," she says, "and you just like slid down the stairs, and when you were walking, you were kind of stumbling, and you just like kind of knocked your shoulder into the wall," she tells me.

I stay quiet and look back at her, occasionally nodding to encourage her to keep going; I'm listening.

"You looked a bit woozy and tired but you were also like, I don't know. When you were talking to me in bed, I realised you were acting a bit sleepy and unnatural cause when I told you to go to bed, you were like *I am in bed* and you also booped Oscar on the nose."

I smile as she tells me about me laying in her bed, thinking it was mine, with our dog. It's uncomfortable for me to hear her talking about a night I don't remember, but I look at her and nod again, so she keeps going.

"It was like totally normal but you never really do that, so I knew something was up as well so I just felt a bit uncomfortable and I was crying because I didn't like it."

My heart is hurting and I hate hearing that I upset her, but I know this is what I need to hear. I need to hear how it made them feel so I have a clear reason never to go back to drinking again and never to allow myself to selfishly put them or myself in harm's way. There are a million different awful scenarios in my head about that night. All the things that could have happened, the dark twists and turns that could have meant we all ended up in a very different place. I feel lucky that we will all heal from this and that I'm getting stronger every day, mentally and emotionally. I'm beginning to believe I can handle this and take on board everything they are saying. I ask Alfie next how he feels about me not drinking anymore.

"I feel good about it," he tells me.

"Why?" I ask.

"Because you're not drunk anymore."

"Do you remember when I was drunk?" I ask. He needs a little more prompting than Olivia to tap into how he feels and what his recollections of my drinking are.

"You were woozy," he says. "You were like stumbling, you were weird and your breath smelled bad. I felt kind of confused."

I ask him if he prefers that I don't drink anymore.

"Yeah," he says.

"How about when adults are drunk around you, how do you feel then?" I ask.

"Also weird," he says, "but like different because they're not my mum."

"So," I go on. "How about when I'm drunk?"

"I feel weird," he says, "confused, sad, annoyed. That sort of stuff."

I'm trying to take it all in, and I'm glad that I'm able to ask these questions and they feel safe enough to answer truthfully, but I also hate hearing how I've made them feel. These are my babies, and I was supposed to be there for them. I'm supposed to protect them. I'm the one who should show them I'm here no matter what and I put them first. I feel like I failed massively.

"Alfie, I'm so sorry you felt like that sweetheart." I mean every word; I'm so sorry.

"It's alright," he tells me.

I look at them both, still holding back my tears. I'm strong, and I want them to know that I've got this for them.

"You don't have to worry about feeling like that again," I tell them. "I promise."

It feels like a weight has been lifted for all of us. They know now that I'm never drinking again, and they tell me how proud they are of me. In the following weeks, they start to notice the changes I'm making and comment on them. Olivia tells me one day after I've been exercising on my Peleton that she thinks it's great; she says, "You used to lay in bed until late and not get up until we had to run to school. Now, you are always up before me, exercising, and seem much happier, especially in the mornings."

It's true; mornings used to be a real struggle. I thought all parents found it hard, and I didn't understand the people who said they got up at 5 am and exercised or made lunches or worked before their kids got up. Now I'm one of them.

I still find mornings hectic and sometimes overwhelming, especially if I've forgotten something like book week, a bake sale, or an excursion. Still, I'm getting better at being organised, present, prepared, and focused.

Since I apologised to the kids, I decide to make amends with everyone. I apologise to Warren first, then my Mum, sister, best friends, friends from uni, and old work colleagues. I even wrote a letter to the mum of my old flatmate whose house I trashed in Chelsea. I remember her coming to me shortly after it happened and being very concerned.

"We're very worried about you," she said. She sat me down opposite her in the lounge of her daughter's little flat on King's Road and asked if I was okay. I wasn't, and I was shaken that she'd taken it upon herself to check in with me when she hardly knew me.

"We are concerned. Is this boy you're seeing good for you?"

I had started seeing a guy I'd met in a club in Clapham. He was a couple of years younger than me and a wine trader. *Trust me to go out with a guy who spent his whole time drinking or selling wine.* I wasn't ok, he was a big drinker and all we seemed to do was go out and get drunk constantly. My friends were worried about me and what a wreck I'd become, but I couldn't see a way out. I thought he loved me and that we were having fun.

My flatmate's mum hugged me, and I collapsed into her lap in floods of tears, "I don't think he's good for me; I don't know what I'm doing," I confessed. I had been desperate to fit in but had managed to ostracise all my friends. I was so touched that she wanted to try and help, but after that, I drifted away from them all because I felt so ashamed. I ended up living with the wine guy and drinking away the next few years of my life.

I wish it had been different, but I wanted her to know how much it meant to me that she tried to help. I had lunch with friends in London and told them how sorry I was. They all said it was ok and that I had just been in a bad place or they hadn't thought anything of it. One friend said she had no idea that I carried on drinking after we left each other at lunch.

"I would go to the supermarket on the way home from meeting you," I confessed. "I would always keep drinking after I started until I blacked out, even when the kids were little."

My friend Naomi looked shocked and sad, "I had no idea, I'm sorry. I wish I'd known so I could have helped."

"It's okay," I tell her sincerely. No one could have helped; I had to help myself. I was the only one who could make me stop, and I had to have a reason to do it. I'm so glad that I finally have one and that the drinking chapter of my life is well and truly over."

Bloated from alcohol abuse

66

Mummy, do you
remember when you
fell? I was crying
because I didn't like
it.

Epilogue

1st March 2024 Brisbane, Australia
882 Days Sober

Something about a library has always made me feel like a different version of myself. I like to imagine playing the lead role as I stroll through the rows and rows of other people's words, all waiting to be discovered inside the covers of their bound homes. I can picture the words that have poured out of someone else and are enshrined here, just waiting to be discovered and brought back into the real world like a genie stuck in a lamp. If I rub the right book, I'll be transported to another world, another person's dream, or someone else's reality.

I like the idea of opening a book and leaving myself behind.

That's what libraries feel like to me: possibility.

I'm tingling with anticipation when I enter Brisbane's state library. I want to be inspired by these words, these completed stories urging me to add my own words to the shelves. I want more than anything for that to become a reality, but I'm still plagued by imposter syndrome and question myself incessantly.

Is my *writing good enough?"* I ask myself.

Can I *do the thing* I've been yearning to do since I was *a child?*

Can I write something worthy of being picked up and read?

Can I bring my story to life and open the door for a reader?

What will they find in my world?

Will they like it and want to stick around for the ending?

I fear that anyone who reads what I'm yet to write will put it down after ten pages and post about it in their Facebook groups and on Instagram, reviewing my work and calling it a bunch of crap.

As I enter the Queensland Writers Centre, I tell the annoying voice in my head to shut up and remind myself that they've deemed my writing worthy. I've been awarded a residency and invited to share their offices to write my story. I locate the feeling I felt when I received the letter telling me I'd won, telling me that I would be their Fishbowl Resident for ten weeks, and latch onto that.

They have an office for me with glass walls that look out into the library and onto the Brisbane River; it is a literal fishbowl. Anyone entering the library can see me setting up my laptop and iPad, putting my Air Pods in and readjusting the seat to find the right position to enable the flow of words to leave my body and land on the page. Students in school uniforms, grandparents with toddlers in tow and tourists glance my way as they browse the aisles of the reference section. I'm sure they wonder what I'm doing and why I would have been placed in a glass box like an art installation. I imagine a plaque on the outside describing what the artist was trying to convey with this piece — *writer at work, creating under the watchful gaze of the ever-present future reader.*

This is the beginning of me telling my story for real, the story of how I turned my life upside down with alcohol and how I managed to put it right side up. I thought this would be a guidebook, a how-to-get-sober manual, but I quickly realised I'm not qualified to advise anyone. I wouldn't take advice from someone who had fucked up as much as I have, even if they have lived to tell the tale. So, telling the tale is what I am qualified to do, and it is what I'm going to do. I've pitched my story, even though I cringed at the thought of writing a memoir. I didn't feel like that was what I wanted. I thought it was embarrassing to write about myself, that it somehow highlighted my lack of creativity and made it evident that I couldn't conjure up characters.

A few months earlier, I sat in the front row of a Mother's Day High Tea as part of the Brisbane Writers Festival. I'd seen authors Holly Wainwright and Francis Whiting discussing Holly's new book. I saw their novels and longed to be like them. I wanted to write; I've always wanted to write, but I didn't know where to start. Even though I have a degree in Journalism and have taken numerous creative writing courses online I've always been derailed by my self-doubt when it came to writing an actual book.

On the morning of the festival, I'm sat with my mum and a group of other mums and daughters, all listening intently and drinking cups of tea. I feel like this is where I should be. I'm full of wonder as I listen to Holly talking about her achievements as if they were so straightforward, achievable and normal. I'm in awe. After she's finished interviewing Holly, Frances asks if there are any questions. My hand shoots up to the sky.

"Yes, you," Frances says, looking my way as I rise from my seat and feel the eyes of the room on me.

"I was just wondering if you had any advice for a budding author?"

"Are you the budding author?" Holly asks as I feel my face flush.

"Um, yes, well, I want to write. I mean, I do write, but I'm a journalist, and I want to write books, so I didn't know if you would recommend any courses or books I could read or you know, something like that." I force myself to stop talking as I feel myself start nervously rambling.

"Yes, you should try one of the courses at the Queensland Writers Centre, "Frances says. "Are you a member?"

"Um, no, not yet, but I've seen their courses, so I will try that; thank you."

"You should read *Bird by Bird* by Anne Lamott," she adds.

"That's a great one," Holly agrees, "Do that and just write, get going."

"Thank you," I say and sit down, feeling relieved.

My mum smiles at me. "You are always so brave asking questions," she says, patting my arm. I feel silly, but I want to know more; I want to pick their brains and discover the secret to being a real writer, not just one who writes the odd article. I want to write books, talk about books and be an author. I get copies of both of their novels so I have another chance to talk to them and join the line to meet Holly. When I reach the front of the queue, and she starts signing my book, I start rambling again.

"So, I want to write, but I can't stop using myself in my writing. I need to make up characters, but I'm struggling."

"What's wrong with writing about yourself?" She probes.

"Well, I guess I didn't want it to all be about me," I say feebly.

"Just use it. Use everyone you know as inspiration; write about what you know, and the rest will come."

I smile and she agrees to pose for a picture with me. I am a complete fangirl and try to commit her wisdom to memory. *Just write what you know*, I repeat in my head. We stand close together and smile as her publisher snaps a picture of us holding up her book.

"Good luck with the writing," her publisher says. "Do send us a pitch when you're ready." I nearly faint. *Is this how it works? Do you meet authors and send publishers pitches?*

I sidle up to Frances, who is also signing copies of her books, and ask if she'll sign mine.

"Here you go," she says, handing it back.

"Thanks for your advice; it means so much."

"You should write for us," she says. "For the magazine. I write for Q Weekend. Do you know Laura, the editor?"

"No," I say,

"Send me an email, and I'll connect you. You can send her some ideas for an article"

"Wow," my mum says as she looks at me, clutching my books on the ferry from the city to home. We bump across the Brisbane River, and I can't wipe the grin off my face. The wind blows my hair, and I feel like I've just been let through the door to the world of books. It's like all I had to do was knock, and I could see every opportunity on the other side just waiting for me.

"I'm going to do it," I tell Mum.

"What, write?" she asks.

"Yes, I'm finally going to write properly. I'm going to write about quitting drinking and how it changed everything."

"That's a fabulous idea; you have so much to share."

That's how I find myself inside the fishbowl, writing out page after page of facts about drinking and alcohol, researching the power of big alcohol companies and talking to people who run rehab centres. I call doctors and researchers, scientists and people who run charities. I interview them for my radio show and write page after page of notes, hoping it will magically transform into a fully formed book and leap out of my computer onto one of the shelves in the library.

I browse the aisles during my breaks from typing, picking out spots where I imagine my book sitting, and then I imagine whole sections full of things I've written. I curse my shoes which are squeaking loudly in the silent concentration of the hushed room, and pretend not to be quite so awkward. I imagine myself as a graceful author with flowing locks, a floaty gown, and non-squeaky shoes. I don't know what I will write about next, but I want this to be my life—typing and wandering around libraries in floaty dresses.

I go downstairs to the open terrace, which is full of school kids on an excursion. I pass the family space and see kids playing in the window seats, books strewn everywhere. I spent so much time in the library with the kids when they were babies. It was one of the only warm places to hide when the temperature dropped in London. When we needed a change of scenery and my foggy brain couldn't deal with the overwhelming noise of the shopping centre or the maritime museum, we headed for the library. I would curl up with them and read as they handed me book after book. Olivia started reading to herself very early, but Alfie liked me to read to him. I still know most of *Where the Wild Things Are* by heart, it was his favourite.

In the library café, I order an oat flat white and a bottle of sparkling water to take back to my desk. As the barista works through the orders before mine, I browse the books in the adjoining shop. There's a massive poster for *Lola in the mirror*, the new book by local author Trent Dalton. I've been listening to it on Audible on my drive into the library and am so in love with this book that I never want it to end. I see the places he writes about on my walks along the river, and I can vividly see his version of Brisbane.

I want to write like that. I pray for some of that creative genius to wash off on me as I listen. I snap a picture of the poster and the display of books and post it on my Instagram stories, tagging Trent in the photo. I caption it, "Writing my book and being inspired by Lola." Trent likes the message and shoots a reply, "Write like the wind Alex." I'm touched and take it as another sign that I'm on the right track. Right here in this library, I'm where I should be, finding the time, space and inspiration to put the words on the page and write my story.

The ten weeks fly by. Sometimes, my fingers can't keep up with the words coming out of me, and other times, I sit staring blankly at my screen. I wander around the office and chat to the other two writers in residence. One is writing a book and a play simultaneously, and another is developing a screenplay. I marvel at their creativity and confidence and try to emulate this when discussing my book project. I can't help feeling awkward and downplaying my work.

The heads of the centre regularly pop their heads around the curtain, which separates the fishbowl from the main open-plan area of the office. Lori-Jay and Anne check in with me and Anne hooks me up with a mentor called Vicki. She's written dozens of books in the same style as mine. We chat about where I want my book to go, and she steers me in a more clearly defined direction. I'm terrified when I send her the first two chapters, but she tells me how much potential it has and that she can tell I have what it takes to write well. Vicki encourages me to take it to the next level, and suddenly, the book has structure, a timeline and a publishing date.

I stick to my writing, putting words down every day. I'm disciplined and motivated in a way I haven't ever felt before. I have momentum that mirrors the drive I have to stay sober. The feeling I'm getting from knowing I'm putting a whole book on paper is only eclipsed by the feeling I have from knowing that giving up drinking got me here. I feel accomplished and brave, but I also wonder why on earth I didn't do it sooner. Why did it take me so long to write these words and to stop drinking?

I spent years not feeling like I was good enough to write anything. I thought nothing I would write would be of any consequence and yet on a Saturday morning in January, I see my face staring out at me from the newspaper. An article I've written about quitting drinking and writing this book is in every newspaper across the country. It's on news websites and all over social media. I'm getting dozens of messages from friends and people I've never met. People start ordering my book before it's even released; they order so many that it shoots onto the top of the list of new books about alcohol. It feels amazing. All I did was stop drinking and write about it.

Why did it take me so long to do this?

I've been sober now for over two years. I've clocked up 29 months without a drink. There have been 882 days I've woken up without a hangover and 21,168 hours I've not wasted getting or being drunk. I have found delight in looking at my sober app and reading my stats as they change hourly. I looked at it daily at the start, but now I rarely do. Weeks pass without me realising another one has gone by and I didn't drink. I'm focused on living my new life, the one where I write, present my radio show and work on TV again. I'm full of ideas and energy. It's like I've started a whole new chapter of my life and it's so different from the last few chapters that it deserves to be a different book.

My home life looks different too. While I've stopped buying wine and now spend my cash trying non-alcoholic alternatives and indulging myself in creating mocktails of an evening, Warren does still drink, and our house is full of alcohol. He's one of those infuriating—I mean lucky—people who can easily take a drink or leave it. He enjoys nice wine and beer and drinks them with his friends and sometimes with clients. He's never needed alcohol in the way that I used to. He has two wine fridges; one is locked and stocked with expensive wines he's collected over the years, and the other has wines that are good but not special occasion good. There's also a bar cabinet full of every spirit known to mankind. We have beautiful decanters and wine glasses for every style imaginable. On the shelf in our kitchen is a bottle of Dom Perignon engraved with the words,

Alex, Will You Marry Me? Waz.

Alcohol has played such a huge part in my life and is still present in my everyday life but it has lost all its appeal for me. While I might be tempted to break into my kids' stash of chocolates, I never consider raiding the bar cabinet or one of the wine fridges.

When we go out for dinner, I used to worry about feeling like I was missing out or get embarrassed asking what non-alcoholic options there were. Now I love it. There are so many different drinks available, and the mocktail list in some places is the same length as the cocktail list.

The only problem I've faced is when we are out with the kids and they want mocktails too. I'm concerned about blurring the line between giving them drinks that are supposed to mimic alcohol and giving them soft drinks. I hope that by modelling an alcohol-free life and talking to them regularly they understand the power alcohol can have and that they can choose not to drink.

I often wonder whether I would have made different choices if I had known more. The blame for my drinking is complex. It was never just about getting drunk regularly or choosing to become dependent on alcohol. It built up over time and got worse when I was struggling and no one could help me. I needed to be in the right place in time to find my way to sobriety.

I haven't found some magical secret to staying sober in the same way there was no secret to writing. I just needed to write. However, I hesitate to declare that to stop drinking, I just had to stop drinking. It comes with a serious number of caveats. I would have been heading for trouble if I had written this book only because I expected to live off the profits or have it turned into a Netflix series or a movie starring Reese Witherspoon.

The success is in the writing itself; in doing it, everything else is a bonus. I had to do it because I wanted to, rather than for fame or money or to escape a job I hated. To give up drinking, I had to choose myself and do it as much for myself as for my family. I needed a push in the right direction from other authors to get writing and from my kids to get sober. Then, I had to believe I was worthy of achieving both. I had to put in the time and commit to these things. There was no magic pill, no secret door at the back of the cupboard, no genie granting my wishes. I had to change everything before everything changed in return.

Once I found my reasons to stop drinking and start writing, I discovered I knew how to do it, and I discovered there is no greater feeling than closing the book on my drinking days and typing the words …

THE END.

Engagement champagne

> I had to change everything before everything changed in return.

Resources

H ere's a list of organisations, websites and services that offer alcohol support, counselling and information in Australia.

Services

Alcohol and Drug Information Service
The Alcohol and Drug Information Service provides 24/7 support for people in Queensland with alcohol and other drug concerns.
1800 177 833
www.adis.health.qld.gov.au

Alcohol. Think Again The 'Alcohol.
Think Again' website provides resources and information about the effects of alcohol on your health. There is information for parents, young people, and women who are pregnant or breastfeeding.
www.alcoholthinkagain.com.au

ASSIST portal
The ASSIST (alcohol, smoking and substance involvement screening test) portal is an easy-to-use tool that detects substance use and related problems. It asks 8 questions and takes about 5 to 10 minutes to complete.
www.assistportal.com.au

DirectLine
Contact DirectLine for confidential alcohol and drug counselling and referral in Victoria Australia. The service is available 24/7 by phone or online.
1800 888 236

eheadspace

eheadspace is a national online and phone support service for young people between 12 and 25. It covers a wide range of topics and issues affecting mental health. Contact them online or by phone from 9am to 1am AEST, every day.

www.headspace.org.au

1800 650 890

Family Drug Support (FDS)

Contact Family Drug Support (FDS) for help dealing with drug and alcohol use in your family. Their free national telephone support line is available 24/7 anywhere in Australia. They also provide support groups, education programs, counselling and bereavement services for families.

www.fds.org.au

1300 368 186

FASD Hub Australia

The FASD Hub provides information about fetal alcohol spectrum disorders (FASD). You can browse a directory of health services and providers with FASD expertise and find details about FASD training for professionals and providers.

www.fasdhub.org.au

Health Direct Hotline

Call this number to speak to a registered nurse about your health concerns. The hotline is open 24 hours a day, 7 days a week.

www.healthdirect.gov.au

1800 022 222

Kids Helpline

Kids Helpline provides a free, private, confidential phone and online counselling service for young people aged 5 to 25. The service is available 24 hours a day from anywhere in Australia.

Kids Helpline 1800 551 800

Positive Choices

Positive Choices is an online portal for teachers, principals, school counsellors, First Nation education officers, youth workers, parents and young people. It aims to raise awareness about the harms associated with alcohol and other drug use by providing tools and school-based programs.
www.positivechoices.org.au

Pregnant Pause

Pregnant Pause provides support to help you and your loved ones go alcohol-free during pregnancy. Having support can make it much easier to stop drinking and give your child the best possible start in life.
www.pregnantpause.com.au

ReachOut

Visit the ReachOut website for help and support on mental health issues for young people. Information is also available for parents and schools.
www.au.reachout.com

Sober in the Country

Sober in the country is a grassroots NFP going "upstream" and changing the narrative around booze in the bush. SITC provides online peer support for rural and remote Australians interested in sobriety to connect.
www.soberinthecountry.org

Drug Information Directory

Use the Drug Information Directory to find information on alcohol and other drugs, including treatment services.

Alcohol and Drug Foundation (ADF)

The Alcohol and Drug Foundation provides facts, resources and programs to help prevent alcohol and other drug harm in Australian communities.
www.adf.org.au
1800 250 015

Drug AwareContact
Drug Aware's 24-hour alcohol and drug support line for help in Western Australia. Their website also provides information about drugs and their impact, and how to stay safe for young people.
Country WA 1800 198 024
City WA 08 9442 5000

Organisations

Alcoholics Anonymous (AA) Australia
To find an AA meeting close to you or for information about quitting or reducing your drinking, contact AA or visit their website.
1300 222 222

Counselling Online
Counselling Online is a free and confidential service that provides 24/7 support to people across Australia affected by alcohol or drug use.
www.counsellingonline.org.au

Drug Strategy
Department of Health and Aged Care
Contact the Drug Strategy team for information about Australia's National Drug Strategy and help with any of its related resources.
www.health.gov.au/resources/collections/national-drug-strategy
enquiries@health.gov.au

Foundation for Alcohol Research and Education (FARE)
Visit the FARE website to find out what they're doing to influence government policy on alcohol. Learn about the alcohol-focused research they support and browse their other resources about alcohol.
www.fare.org.au

Hello Sunday Morning

Offers free tools for Australians who want to take a break, cut back or quit drinking. Daybreak is an anonymous online peer support community with thousands of members. The self-assessment screener helps you decide what support you need. A newsletter also offers inspiration to stay on track.
www.hellosundaymorning.org

Lifeline

Contact Lifeline for support if you are experiencing a personal crisis or have suicidal thoughts. You can call them 24 hours a day, 7 days a week from anywhere in Australia for crisis support. You can also send a text message or contact their confidential online chat.
24-hour crisis line 131 114
www.lifeline.org.au

National Centre for Education and Training on Addiction (NCETA)

NCETA aims to help organisations and workers to better respond to problems related to alcohol and other drugs (AOD). Find out about their research into intervention programs for workplaces and effective workforce development.
www.nceta.flinders.edu.au

National Drug and Alcohol Research Centre (NDARC)

NDARC conducts research into alcohol and other drug (AOD) treatment. Find up-to-date information about AOD treatment options and how effective they are at reducing AOD-related harm.
www.ndarc.med.unsw.edu.au

National Drug Research Institute (NDRI)

NDRI conducts research that contributes to effective alcohol and other drug (AOD) policies, strategies, and practices. Browse its latest publications and resources and read about its research programs.
www.ndri.curtin.edu.au

Index

A

abuse xix
addicted 82
Addicted 1
addiction xv, xvi, xxi, 2, 6
ADHD 75
affirmation 64
alcohol xi, 52
alcoholic 45
alcoholism 6, 8, 15, 77
Amends 107
anxiety 77, 90
Anxiety 11
ASD 75
attention 75
Australia 23, 32, 64
Australian Bureau of Statistics xvi
Australian Department of Health, xv

B

beginning 120
booze 61
booze, xvii
break 58
Break 43
Brisbane 63, 69, 85

C

Cavalier King Charles 64
Centre for Alcohol Policy Research xv

www.ingramcontent.com/pod-product-compliance
Lightning Source LLC
Chambersburg PA
CBHW060052100426
42742CB00014B/2788